# Moral Perception

SOOCHOW UNIVERSITY LECTURES IN PHILOSOPHY
Chienkuo Mi, General Editor

The Soochow University Lectures in Philosophy are given
annually at Soochow University in Taiwan by leading
international figures in contemporary analytic philosophy.

*Also in the series:*

Scott Soames, *What Is Meaning?*
Ernest Sosa, *Knowing Full Well*

# Moral Perception

Robert Audi

PRINCETON UNIVERSITY PRESS

PRINCETON AND OXFORD

Published by Princeton University Press, 41 William Street,
Princeton, New Jersey 08540
In the United Kingdom: Princeton University Press, 6 Oxford Street,
Woodstock, Oxfordshire OX20 1TW

press.princeton.edu

Library of Congress Cataloging-in-Publication Data

Audi, Robert, date.
Moral perception / Robert Audi.
p. cm. — (Soochow University lectures in philosophy)
Includes bibliographical references and index.
ISBN 978-0-691-15648-4 (hardcover : alk. paper) 1. Ethics.
2. Perception. I. Title.
BJ1031.A93 2013
170'.42—dc23
2012027521

British Library Cataloging-in-Publication Data is available

This book has been composed in Minion Pro

Printed on acid-free paper. ∞

Printed in the United States of America

1 3 5 7 9 10 8 6 4 2

# Contents

*Preface*  vii

*Acknowledgments*  xi

INTRODUCTION  1

PART ONE
*Perception and Moral Knowledge*  5

CHAPTER 1
*Perception: Sensory, Conceptual,
and Cognitive Dimensions*  7
I. Major Kinds of Perception  8
II. The Phenomenology and Content of Perception  12
III. The Basis of Veridical Perception  21

CHAPTER 2
*Moral Perception: Causal, Phenomenological, and
Epistemological Elements*  30
I. The Perception of Right and Wrong  30
II. The Representational Character of Moral Perception  38

CHAPTER 3
*Perception as a Direct Source of Moral Knowledge*  51
I. Perception and Inference  51
II. Can Moral Perception Be Naturalized?  55
III. Moral Perception as a Basis of Moral Knowledge  58

PART TWO
*Ethical Intuition, Emotional Sensibility,
and Moral Judgment*  67

CHAPTER 4
*Perceptual Grounds, Ethical Disagreement,
and Moral Intuitions*  69

I. Does Moral Disagreement Undermine Justification in Ethics?  70
II. The Concept of an Intuition  83
III. Intuitions as Apprehensions  96

CHAPTER 5
*Moral Perception, Aesthetic Perception,
and Intuitive Judgment*  103

I. The Role of Intuition in Aesthetic Experience  103
II. Aesthetic and Moral Properties: Comparison and Contrast  106
III. The Rule-Governed Element in Ethics and Aesthetics  109
IV. The Reliability of Intuition  112

CHAPTER 6
*Emotion and Intuition as Sources of Moral Judgment*  121

I. Emotion and Intuition: Interaction and Integration  122
II. The Evidential Role of Emotion in Moral Matters  136

CHAPTER 7
*The Place of Emotion and Moral Intuition
in Normative Ethics*  143

I. Emotion and Moral Intuition  143
II. Moral Imagination as a Nexus of Intuition,
Emotion, and Perception  157
III. Intuition and Moral Judgment  161

CONCLUSION  170

*Index*  175

# Preface

THIS BOOK WAS PREPARED for the Soochow Lectures in Philosophy and, in an earlier, shorter version, presented at Soochow University in Taipei in March 2011. The Soochow series is intended to stand as a source of continuing contributions to philosophy and a setting for establishing fruitful connections between philosophers in Taiwan and many other philosophers worldwide. Even beyond those connections, the series aims at stimulating interchanges of ideas between philosophers working in Chinese and those working in other languages. With this context in mind, I have selected a topic that spans three very broad areas and should interest philosophers and others working in any of these fields: ethics, both theoretical and practical; epistemology, conceived as the theory of knowledge *and* justification; and moral psychology, conceived as inquiry in the areas of overlap between philosophy of mind and ethical theory. The book is intended to engage the interests of philosophers and other thinkers working in any of these areas.

Every chapter has been greatly expanded since its partial presentation in Taipei, but I have retained the concreteness and the numerous examples needed for comprehension by an audience that lacked the text. My aim continues to be a high level of readability such that students as well as professional readers can readily follow the argument. Copious notes are included for those interested in certain qualifications or in references to relevant literature, but the notes are not needed for understanding the major points.

The main ideas in the book should be comprehensible to readers who skip or merely consult Chapter 1, which is perhaps the most complex. Chapter 1 is required for any defense and full-scale understanding of Chapter 2 and later chapters, but those are sufficiently clarified by examples of their main points to be intelligible apart from it. Readers interested in ethics but not epistemology, then, might try reading the introduction and proceeding directly to Chapter 2. To some extent, *any* chapter, but especially 7, may be understood by itself. Chapter 7 may certainly be taught on its own by an instructor with an understanding of the work as a whole.

It is appropriate here to say something about the contribution of the book in each of the fields within its scope. Perception is a basic topic. My account of it draws on years of work on the subject but is presented here in a self-contained treatment and with footnotes indicating much relevant literature. This book will show how the account can accommodate the idea that perception occurs in the moral domain. Much will be said about perception in Chapter 1, with many examples drawn from the domain of vision. Perception is not only basic for success in everyday life and scientific inquiry; it is essential for moral knowledge and crucial for cross-cultural understanding. It is the common root that nourishes our cognitive structure; it anchors that structure to the grounds from which truth emerges; and it sustains the vast and various superstructures we build from the foundational materials that perception provides. If there is moral perception, and if some of our sound moral beliefs suitably rest on it, then there is moral knowledge.

On the basis of the account of perception outlined in the first chapter, Chapters 2 and 3 present a theory of moral perception and represent it as an important element in moral life. In stressing the importance of perception for understanding in ethics, I am not suggesting—and do not believe—that all moral knowledge is perceptual. This point raises the question of how nonperceptual moral knowledge is related to perception, a question pursued in Chapters 4 and 5. I am especially interested in intuitive moral knowledge—whose existence I have argued for in *The Good in the Right: A Theory of Intuition and Intrinsic Value* (Princeton University Press, 2004)—and in the ways in which intuitive moral knowledge is connected with perception and emotion. These concerns are explored in detail in Chapters 6 and 7. The role of moral imagination in relation to all three of these—perception, intuition, and emotion—is also an important topic in this inquiry and is discussed in Chapter 7.

A central concern of the book is the issue of objectivity in ethics. From that point of view, the influence of emotion on moral cognition is a major topic. A common assumption is that emotions bias us and undermine objectivity. Doubtless they can do this, but I will show how they can also have evidential value and thereby contribute to our moral knowledge and, more broadly, to our ethical sensitivity and to the refinement and justification of various important elements in our moral outlook.

The book does not challenge moral skepticism directly, but if the account of perception and its relation to moral judgment is sound, the common-sense view that we have a good deal of knowledge in ethical matters gains support. Even those who reject that view will be able to see how perception can at least provide some degree of rational support for moral judgment.

Intuition can be similarly seen to have evidential value, even if it is not taken to constitute knowledge or to provide evidence sufficient for knowledge. And emotion can be seen—at least in people of maturity and discernment—not as a threat to objectivity but, under many conditions, as a basis for justified moral judgment.

# Acknowledgments

THIS BOOK HAS BENEFITED FROM DISCUSSIONS with more people than I can name. These include both philosophers and students of philosophy. For comments on earlier versions of all or part of the book I want to thank Carla Bagnoli, Roger Crisp, Jonathan Dancy, Peter J. Graham, Scott Hagaman, Terry Horgan, Chris Howard, Ralph Kennedy, Justin McBrayer, Hugh McCann, Chienkuo Mi, Walter Sinnott-Armstrong, Ernest Sosa, Pekka Vyrynen, Dennis Whitcomb, readers for the Press, and, especially, Robert C. Roberts and Mark C. Timmons, who both took time to make a great many detailed helpful points.

Discussions with Paul Audi, John Broome, Maeve Cook, Miranda Fricker, the late Peter Goldie, Darcia Narvaez, Derek Parfit, Peter Railton, and Linda Zagzebski have also been of help to me, and I learned much from discussing one or another of the issues with participants in the Soochow Lecture sessions in 2011, the Brackenridge Symposium in 2010 (a conference skillfully organized at the University of Texas, San Antonio by Jill Graper Hernandez and focused on my work), and a seminar at the University of Notre Dame.

The support and advice of my editor at the Press, Rob Tempio, have been invaluable, and I am also grateful for the highly professional editorial work of Lauren Lepow and for help with the index given by Daniel Immerman.

The relation of this book to my earlier work is indicated by various footnotes. None of the chapters is a reprint of any earlier publication, and revisions (sometimes substantial or accompanied by considerable development) have been made in the parts of my previous publications that appear here.

Moral Perception

# Introduction

A PERENNIAL QUEST OF PHILOSOPHY is to construct an adequate conception of the human person and to frame sound standards for human conduct. In the domain of ethics, standards of interpersonal conduct are central. Ethical conduct is essential for human civilization, and in our globalized world, with its increasing international interdependence, nothing is more important than universal adherence to sound ethical standards. Is there any moral knowledge that can serve as a basis for such standards? That is one of the broad questions motivating this book.

With the successes and intellectual prominence of modern science, philosophers and many others who think about the status of ethics have been concerned with the apparent disparity between our ways of arriving at moral judgments and our ways of arriving at beliefs and judgments by using scientific methods. A great many contemporary academics and others maintain—or simply presuppose—that if we have any moral knowledge, that knowledge must be broadly empirical and ultimately amenable to scientific confirmation. This view is implicit in the most common kind of contemporary naturalism. Much could be said about what counts as naturalism, and Chapter 3 will explore the extent to which my theory of moral perception may be considered naturalistic. For our purposes, it is sufficient to bear in mind a wide conception of naturalism. In very broad terms, we might think of it as the position that, first, nature—conceived as the physical universe—is all there is; second, the only basic truths are truths of nature; and, third, the only substantive knowledge is of natural facts.[1] Science, of course, is taken by naturalists to be the highest authority concerning what the truths of nature are.

Naturalism as most commonly conceived contrasts not only with supernaturalistic theism but also with epistemological rationalism. In outline, rationalism in epistemology is the view that the proper use of reason, independently of confirmation from sense experience, yields substantive knowledge (as opposed to knowledge of logical or analytic propositions). A robust rationalism extends to including certain sorts of moral knowledge as among the substantive kinds that may be described as a priori.[2] Such knowledge, though not *unscientific*, is *non*-scientific. There is, however, a major point of important agreement between rationalists and naturalists, even those naturalists who are empiricists. It is that perception is a major source of possible knowledge of its

---

[1] Detailed discussion of what constitutes naturalism and whether normative notions, such as obligation and intrinsic goodness, can be naturalized is provided in my "Can Normativity Be Naturalized?" in *Ethical Naturalism: Current Debates*, ed. Susana Nuccetelli and Gary Shea (Cambridge: Cambridge University Press, 2012), 169–93.

[2] How rationalism may be conceived is discussed, and the position defended, in my "Skepticism about the A Priori: Self-Evidence, Defeasibility, and *Cogito* Propositions," in *The Oxford Handbook of Skepticism*, ed. John Greco (Oxford: Oxford University Press, 2008), 149–75; and how rationalism applies to moral knowledge is indicated in chaps. 1 and 2 of my *The Good in the Right: A Theory of Intuition and Intrinsic Value* (Princeton, NJ: Princeton University Press, 2004).

objects and that any genuine knowledge of the physical universe depends on perception.

My main project in this book is to show how perception figures in giving us moral knowledge and how moral perception is connected with intuition and emotion. In showing this, I will combat stereotypes regarding both intuition and emotion, especially the view that they are either outside the rational order or tainted by irrationality.[3] In doing this, I will at many points criticize one or another form of *intellectualism*. By this I mean the tendency to treat perception, cognition (especially belief formation), and rationality itself as dependent on intellectual operations such as inference, reasoning processes, and analysis. Rationality is not intellectuality, and intellectual activity is not entailed by rationality in belief, action, judgment, or other elements that may be appraised in the dimensions of truth or rationality.

More broadly still, I hope to realize two complementary aims: to lay out major elements of a moral philosophy that reflects a well-developed epistemology and to make epistemological points that emerge best in exploring the possibility of moral knowledge. I try to do this from the perspective of a philosophy of mind that makes it possible to understand human agency and cognition with minimal posits: roughly, without burdening the mental life of rational persons—and doubtless our brains—any more than necessary for understanding the data. Here I join forces

---

[3] Here my concerns overlap those of Jonathan Haidt in his much-discussed work on social intuitionism, "The Emotional Dog and Its Rational Tail: A Social Intuitionist View of Moral Judgment," *Psychological Review* 108 (2001): 814–34, and related work by developmental psychologists who study ethics. For the latter, see, e.g., Darcia Narvaez and Daniel K. Lapsley, eds., *Personality, Identity, and Character: Explorations in Moral Psychology* (Cambridge: Cambridge University Press, 2009).

with many colleagues in neuroscience and with many philosophers holding views more naturalistic than mine. In this spirit, and from the standpoint of both epistemology and philosophy of mind, I aim at clarifying both the nature of intuition and emotion and their evidential role in yielding justified moral judgments and moral knowledge. In doing this, especially in Chapters 4–7, which concern the ethically important interconnections among perception, intuition, and emotion, I will identify some of the main standards of the normative ethics that seems to me most plausible.

If this overall project succeeds in the way I intend, it provides a foundation for affirming the possibility of moral knowledge that is, on the one hand, based on perception and hence empirical and, on the other hand, comprehensible in terms of a framework of a priori moral principles that are not empirical and are knowable by reflection. Moral philosophy spans the empirical and a priori domains, and I shall argue that it does so in a way that makes possible both objective moral judgments and cross-cultural communication in ethics.

# PART ONE

*Perception and Moral Knowledge*

CHAPTER 1

# Perception: Sensory, Conceptual, and Cognitive Dimensions

PERCEPTION IS CENTRAL IN EPISTEMOLOGY, and the concept of perception is among the most important in philosophy. No one doubts that perception is essential for human knowledge, and we trust its deliverances. If there is dispute about whether someone pointed a laser beam at an airplane in flight, honest testimony that one *saw* the act normally settles the dispute. It is even common for people to go so far as to say that seeing is believing. The prominence of this adage indicates the importance that visual perception is taken to have for grounding belief and knowledge. The sense of touch is also highly trusted. If I feel my wallet in my pocket as I move through a crowd, I am confident that it is in fact there. Indeed, tactile perception may have even greater psychological authority than any of the other senses. If, looking at my wallet in my hand, I suddenly ceased to see it but could feel it in my grip, I would likely fault my vision rather than my sense of touch. Whatever we might conclude about the relative power that different modes of perception have over cognition, the clear and steadfast deliverances of visual perception—which is the main kind of perception considered here—are not easily overridden.

If the psychological authority of perception—chiefly its power to compel belief under varying conditions—is not in general contested, its epistemic authority—chiefly its power to yield knowledge and justified belief—is often taken to be limited to certain realms and to hold for descriptive rather than normative propositions. Paradigms of the former are propositions ascribing observable properties, such as color and shape, to macroscopic objects. Related to these propositions are those ascribing to objects of scientific concern properties of the kinds needed for explanations in the natural sciences. Paradigms of normative propositions are those ascribing obligations to persons, wrongness to actions, or intrinsic goodness or badness to states of affairs.

There are many people, in and outside philosophy, who, taking descriptive propositions to exhaust what is perceptually knowable, think that perception does not yield moral knowledge. Commonly, such moral skeptics believe that perception bears on settling moral disagreements only when they turn on differences over "facts" such as those observable in the scientific study of behavior. Assessment of this skeptical view about the status of ethics requires both an account of perception and an understanding of the nature and basis of perceptual moral judgments. The former topic will be central in this chapter, the latter in the next.

## I. Major Kinds of Perception

The term 'perception' is quite abstract and presents a challenge to philosophical analysis. But there is no controversy about whether paradigms of perception include certain experiences in the five ordinary sensory modes: seeing, hearing, touching, tasting, and smelling. We should not, however, consider this list of perceptual modes exhaustive. For one thing, it omits proprioception, for instance certain kinds of direct awareness of bodily processes, which, like an awareness of tensing muscles, might be considered a kind of inner perception. There are also significant differences among the perceptual modes on the list; but at least in philosophy, seeing is the favorite paradigm of perception. My aim will be to make points about perception that have wide application, but it will simplify discussion to use mainly visual examples and some auditory cases involving reception of speech acts.

In addition to perceptual seeing, there is seeing in the intellective, apprehensional sense. Seeing that realism in ethics is controversial is an important element in understanding philosophical discussions, but it is not perceptual seeing. Similarly, seeing an American flag displayed daily on a residential porch might be viewed, and in that sense seen, as an indication of a political position, but, unlike seeing a stick half-sunk in water as bent, this is not perceptual seeing *as*. As these cases illustrates, one liability of focusing on seeing is conflating perceptual with intellective seeing. If the distinction is not sharp, it is clear enough to enable us to distinguish intellectual moral seeing (such as seeing that we ought not to cheat others) from the moral perceptions that concern me. Another case of seeing is "seeing in the mind's eye," a kind of imaginational seeing. That is best treated as an instance of visual imagination, which is morally significant in ways described in Chapters 6 and 7. It is possible even given blindness. It is not perceptual.

It will help to begin with three main cases of perceptual seeing: (1) seeing an object, such as a log in a fireplace; (2) seeing an object to have a property, say seeing a log to be smoldering; and (3) seeing that some "observational" proposition holds, for instance that a face is tanned. I call these *simple perception, attributive perception,* and *propositional perception.*[1] All three manifest the veridicality—the *factivity*—of perception.

Let me illustrate. First, if I see a face, there *is* in fact a face that I see; this illustrates *referential* factivity. The point is not that perception itself makes a reference, though a rationale for saying so is plain in such cases; but in specifying what someone perceived *we* must make a reference, and it will be to something real. Second—to proceed to a different way of ascribing a perception—if I see a face *to be* bearded, there is a face that I in fact see *and it is bearded.* This illustrates both referential and *attributive* factivity—*predicative* factivity, in a terminology I take to be roughly equivalent. There must be something I perceive and, if I see it to be bearded (and so I implicitly attribute—or at least my perceptual system implicitly attributes—beardedness to it), then it is bearded.[2] Third, suppose I *see that* that face is bearded. Then this proposition is true. This case illustrates *propositional* factivity: in effect, I see the truth of a proposition (loosely, I see that a proposition is true). Normally, I also *know* the proposition in question to be true.

These points about perception are apparently conceptual. Reflection will show that someone's using perceptual language in

---

[1] Here and in discussing perception generally I draw on chap. 1 of my *Epistemology*, 3rd ed. (New York: Routledge, 2010). I have, however, substituted 'attributive' for 'objectual' with the idea that the former is more intuitive and can serve the same function.

[2] At least normally, seeing a thing to have a property *F* entails seeing its *F*-ness. If so, predicative seeing is also a case of simple seeing of a property, and predicative seeing might plausibly be viewed as a special case of referential factivity.

a way that presupposes their falsehood would be strong prima facie evidence of misunderstanding perceptual concepts. What, then, of someone said to "see ghosts?" Such special uses of 'see' normally indicate ascriptions of visual experience without an external object and may be set aside here. When people are said to see ghosts, it is normally presupposed that this is not genuinely perceiving them but is, or is akin to, hallucinating them.

Very commonly, we not only see things but also see them as something definite. One usually sees a ship not as a mere hulk—as one might if one were next to it in a rowboat looking at just one side—but as a many-faceted conveyance with a base and superstructure. Conceptually, seeing *as* is two-dimensional: there is the thing seen, for instance a spruce, and the set of properties it is seen as having, say being windblown. Seeing *as* is a hybrid notion. This is because, at least in perceptual cases (the kind that concern us), seeing *as* is veridical and referential as to the object that is seen—here it is like simple seeing—but neither necessarily veridical nor referentially transparent as to what is, as it were, visually predicated. In the first, referential dimension, then, it is like simple seeing; in the second, attributive dimension, it differs both from simple seeing and from attributive seeing, which is veridical in the predicative dimension. Consider a child's seeing a stuffed hound as a lion. This entails that there *is* a stuffed hound seen, but not that a lion is seen. The *as*-phrase may be followed by a term for something merely imagined.

Seeing *as*, moreover, is also not transparent; i.e., it may fail to apply even if we substitute a true description for one indicating the aspect of the object the perceiver focuses on. Someone who sees a tabletop as circular need not see it as having the shape of a figure whose circumference is pi times its diameter, even though these terms necessarily designate the same things.[3] The position of the expression following 'as', then, is neither necessarily factive (as shown by the stuffed hound case) nor referentially transparent (as indicated by the table case).[4]

Much more could be said about simple, attributive, and propositional perception, but the points I have made enable us to proceed to other aspects of perception and then, in Chapter 2, to the nature and status of moral perception.

## II. The Phenomenology and Content of Perception

For both epistemological and metaphysical reasons, it is important to examine the phenomenology of perception. We may plausibly assume that perception is experiential. To see (or otherwise perceive) entails having an experience, and the experience is distinctively qualitative. To illustrate the phenomenal sense, there is something it is *like* to see a yellow grapefruit and something it is like to feel its surface. Here 'like' has its phenomenal sense, not its comparative sense. A child can know what it is like to feel the surface of a grapefruit even if, before this occasion, the child has

[3] These examples suggest that seeing *as* is conceptual. But that does not follow, and I leave open that in some cases it is not. Non-transparency is necessary but not sufficient for the conceptual character of the position following 'as' in such locutions, and there may be ways of seeing *x* as *F* that, without conceptualization, simply require a determinate way of responding to something's being *F*.

[4] Seeing *as* may be cognitive rather than perspectival; but our subject is perceptual rather than intellective, seeing *as*, e.g. doxastic seeing *as*, in which the perceiver *believes* the object has the property it is seen as having. In part because seeing *as* does not meet the factivity standard applicable to attributive and propositional seeing, I will not discuss it in detail in relation to moral perception. The three factive cases are also more important for the epistemology of perception.

never felt anything else with a similar surface.[5] Knowing what something is like, in the phenomenal sense, is a matter of the content of consciousness understood as object(s) of awareness; it does not require knowing what something *else* is like and knowing the former to share some property with the latter.

## The Representational Element in Perception

Perception is not only experiential but also in *some* sense "representational." If it is indeed factive in the way illustrated—implying certain truths—a natural assumption would be that it represents its object: the thing that is (e.g.) seen and (normally) seen to have, and in that way represented as having, some property. The perceiver may also see *that* the object has a property. But seeing that something is so entails believing that it is so,[6] and simple

---

[5] Doubtless there can be "blindsight," understood as a "direct" cognitive response to visible properties unaccompanied by relevant visual experience. But a person incapable of visual experience could have that; even a mechanical robot could, if it could have knowledge at all. We need not call either kind of knowledge a case of seeing that something is so. Not all knowledge of the visible is *visual knowledge.* For a discussion of blindsight that contrasts with mine, especially in giving a lesser role—if any essential role—to conscious elements as conditions for genuine seeing, see Tyler Burge, *Origins of Objectivity* (Oxford: Oxford University Press, 2010), esp. 374–75 (his note 10 cites many recent scientific studies of blindsight).

[6] Could a skeptic suspend judgment? The skeptic could well believe a second-order judgment to the effect that the proposition apparently seen to be true might be false. But this is not a counterexample, nor would we expect (non-suicidal) skeptics who see that a bus is bearing down on them to doubt the impending danger. It should be stressed that seeing *x* to *be F* has much in common with seeing that *x* is *F* and can explain much of the behavior explainable by the latter. But the former does not entail the latter, and their similarity does not show that propositional seeing does not entail *believing* the proposition in question.

perception, at least—just perceiving an object—apparently does not entail having any belief about the object.

The representationality of perception is confirmed by the functional dependence—a kind of *discriminative dependence*—of the phenomenal element in perception upon the object perceived. My perceptual experience depends on the perceived object and varies systematically with certain changes in that object. Normally, if the tree that I see is windblown, my visual impression varies with the waving of its branches; if I am perceptually conscious of my chair and it vibrates as a passing train rumbles by, I have a tactile sense of vibrations; in thickening smoke, my olfactory sensations intensify; and so forth. This does not imply that we see visible properties of objects by *seeing* corresponding phenomenal properties. The relation between seeing visible properties of an object and seeing the object itself is not instrumental, and the relevant point for the phenomenology of vision is that seeing the physical properties entails the perceiver's *instantiating*, not seeing, certain of the phenomenal properties.

Given the representationality of perception and the typically rich information it provides to the perceiver, it has become common to speak of perceptual content. This terminology needs clarification. If you see a deer, is the perceived *object* the animal itself—which is in some way *in* the experience—the main content of your experience, or is that content simply a representation of the animal? Are the *properties* you see the animal to have the content of your experience? Does the *proposition* that there is a deer in the field (if you see that there is one there) belong to that content? Do all three of these elements taken together constitute that content?

Perhaps we might say that all the properties phenomenally represented in a perceptual experience constitute its content, given the intuitive sense in which the content of something is what is in it, and given that what is most clearly "in" an experience is the properties, such as color, shape, and sound, that one is sensorily (as opposed to intellectively) aware of. Not all of these properties, however, need belong to the object: a deer seen to be still, which it is, may also be seen as gray, which is it not. We could thus speak of veridical content, which is genuinely perceptual, and sensory content, which need not be or (as is typical with "veridical hallucination") is accidentally so.

To achieve clarity here, we need names. Loosely speaking, we might call the perceived object the *objectual content* of the experience. This would be a kind of external content; but it is "in" the experience, if we conceive genuine perception as partly a relation to the external world. The object is one term in that relation. Thus, a prancing deer before me that fills my visual consciousness might be considered a kind of content of my perceptual experience. The deer might also be conceived as the object that fills my consciousness. Similarly, we might call the phenomenally represented properties—those properties one is in some way conscious of in the perceptual experience—the *property content* of the experience; and we might call the property-ascriptive propositions the perceiver normally can perceptually know on the basis of the perception its *total propositional content*.[7]

[7] We should also distinguish, as in the case of property content, *perceptual* propositional content from *sensory* propositional content. Macbeth's hallucination of a dagger has the latter but not, in my terminology, the former. To be sure, he might have had a mixed experience: hallucinating a dagger while actually seeing the wall before which it seems to hover. Then his overall visual experi-

The propositional content could be divided into at least two kinds. Call any propositions that are perceptually *believed* on the basis of the experience the *doxastic propositional content* of the experience and those propositions that the perceiver is disposed to believe (but does not in fact believe) on the basis of the phenomenal perceptual elements of the experience the *implicit propositional content*. These two categories together may or may not include all the propositions whose truth would make the experience, in respect of its phenomenal content, veridical, i.e., an objectively correct representation of some part of the world.[8] If the experience represents two birds perched on a telephone wire before me, its propositional content includes the proposition that there are two birds on a telephone wire before me; if it represents a yellow dot in a blue patch, it includes the proposition that there is a yellow dot in a blue patch before me; and so forth.[9] These three broad kinds of content, property content and the two propositional kinds, are not the only elements one might take as

---

ence would have both kinds of propositional content. Detailed discussion of the content of visual experience (much of it consistent with the view taken here) is provided by Susanna Siegel in *The Contents of Experience* (Oxford: Oxford University Press, 2010).

[8] Arguably, all such propositions would be included if the person had sufficient conceptual sophistication to believe or be disposed to believe every proposition attributing to the perceptual object some property of it that appropriately figures in the perceptual experience.

[9] Here one might think of the speckled hen problem. If I perceive such a creature, are all the speckles I in some sense see represented in my experience? Perhaps exactly 100 could be visually represented in my perceptual experience. It does not follow that I am even disposed to believe there are 100. There is much to say here, but we need not solve the problem. It is enough to note that anyone who posits propositional content of the kind described need not say either that the subject can *know* by introspection how many speckles there are or that the attempt to determine it will not change the number that are phenomenally "visible."

contents of perception, but they are major elements meriting that name. It will be the property content of moral perception that most concerns us.

### *"Seeing is believing"*

This is a good place to examine the incalculably influential but rarely examined adage "Seeing is believing." This is often taken to mean that if we perceptually see some object or event, we then believe that it exists; but it might also be thought to mean that if we see *that* something is so, we believe that it is. Achieving a good understanding of this adage is perhaps even more important for moral perception than for perception in general. Consider the paragraph you are reading. Do you believe that it is not in longhand or that it has more than four words? Well, you could see that these things are true before I asked. Must you not "believe your eyes?" Now, for *every* property clearly present in your visual field, you might be thought to believe that the object you see bears that property: say, being white, printed (rather than handwritten), appearing in a rectangular block, and having white margins. This idea regarding belief-formation might underlie, and might seem to support, the view that the content of a visual experience is manifested in *beliefs* of all the propositions ascribing the visually represented properties (at least all such propositions one can understand).

This idea inflates the doxastic content of the mind—what one believes—far beyond plausibility. You need not believe—before I mention the point—that this paragraph has more than four words, even if, in merely looking at it, you see many more than four. By virtue of seeing the full paragraph, you are, however, *dis-*

*posed* to believe this. If the matter arises, as where someone has said that she thought the page in question had, as its paragraphs, only four-word short aphorisms, you are likely to believe that this paragraph has more. I contend that it is only under certain conditions that seeing entails (propositional) believing. Apparently, it is mainly where what is seen, or an aspect of it, has some significance for the perceiver that seeing a property of the thing produces the corresponding property-ascriptive belief. Seeing may not produce belief even when one has the relevant thing in view.[10]

One may even *focally* perceive something, as we do the letters we type, without believing, for each, that it is a *t*, that it is a *y*, that it is a *p*, etc. One may also merely *peripherally* perceive something, as where, concentrating on birds in flight, I see but pay no attention to a helicopter flying past them in the distance, and perhaps see it as having some property, such as rising. Focal perception may tend to yield belief, but need not; and merely peripheral perception may tend not to yield it, but may. What should be uncontroversial is that, for those with the appropriate concepts, perception commonly disposes them to form some beliefs and *can* enable them to form indefinitely many that constitute knowledge.

Even when perception produces belief, that belief need not be propositional, as opposed to predicative. Consider seeing a recently harvested Christmas tree. I could believe *it* to be well-

---

[10] For a case supporting the distinction in question, see my "Dispositional Beliefs and Dispositions to Believe," *Nous* 28 (1994): 419–34. Concerning the relation between seeing and believing, consider the locutions 'I could not believe my eyes' and 'I could hardly believe my eyes'. Both indicate how difficult it is to *resist* believing a proposition that comes to mind *and* seems to one (visually) to be true. Shakespeare's Othello demanded the "ocular proof" of Desdemona's infidelity. He surely must have thought that seeing is believing—or the surest kind of believing. (Unfortunately all he saw was an ostensibly incriminating handkerchief.)

proportioned but not believe a *proposition* to the effect that *the recently harvested tree before me* is well-proportioned. For although I *am* seeing a recently harvested tree, I think that it is a plastic imitation bought by my environmentally sensitive hosts. It also seems—and this will later emerge as important for moral perception—that we can *respond* to a property of something, such as a high obstacle in our path which we automatically step over, without *believing* it to have that property. Discriminating the property, such as the height of the obstacle, may suffice to guide our steps so that we do not trip. I doubt that perception can guide behavior *only* through producing guiding beliefs.[11]

These points may be generalized to other perceptual modes. First, we cannot properly understand perception if we overintellectualize it in the way that, perhaps partly because of misunderstanding of the idea that seeing is believing, is natural for many philosophers.[12] Second, it is crucial for understanding both

---

[11] The points made here are supported in my "Justifying Grounds, Justified Beliefs, and Rational Acceptance," in *Rationality and the Good: Critical Essays on the Ethics and Epistemology of Robert Audi*, ed. Mark Timmons, John Greco, and Alfred R. Mele (Oxford: Oxford University Press, 2007), esp. 230–39, which replies to Timothy Williamson's "On Being Justified in One's Head," 106–22. I might add here that how loose we can allow conceptualization to be depends on whether we are thinking of *de dicto* or only *de re* belief. My suggestion is that one need not even *believe* a rock to be slippery in order to respond to its slippery appearance by sidestepping it; but suppose explaining this response does require positing the agent's *believing* it *to be* slippery. That entails property attribution, but does it require the agent's conceptualizing slipperiness? I doubt that, but certainly the discriminative response in question is a likely stage in developing a concept of slipperiness, and some might consider the *de re* belief to require conceptualization of the property it ascribes.

[12] In places Thomas Reid seems to take visual perception to entail belief regarding the object. He says, e.g., in his *Inquiry into the Principles of Common Sense*, "the perception of an object implies both a conception of its form and a belief of its present existence." See Ronald E. Beanblossom and Keith Lehrer, eds., *Thomas Reid: Inquiry and Essays* (Indianapolis, IN: Hackett, 1983), 84. He also says, "My belief is carried along by perception, as irresistibly as my body by

belief—including moral belief—and its justification that we understand how experience, especially perceptual experience, can justify belief or render it knowledge. Believing that this paper is white is justified by my visual experience of white (or, arguably, by my actually *seeing* its whiteness). *Saying* that I see that this paper is white, as some would in justifying this belief to a skeptic, self-ascribes this visual experience and thereby suffices to express my justification; but when I *specify* what justifies this belief, my self-ascription of seeing its whiteness, or of seeing *that* it is white, misleadingly suggests that I must believe that *I see* its whiteness in order to be justified in believing simply *that it is white*. In the order of justification, seeing is prior to its ascription, and perception can provide justification and produce knowledge whether or not we believe it to occur.

## The Causal Element in Perception

My stress on the discriminative dependence of phenomenal perceptual representation on the object perceived should indicate that I regard perception as (or at least as embodying) a causal relation. I am suggesting a causal (and adverbial) theory of perception. On this theory, to perceive something is, in outline, for it to produce or sustain, in the right way, an appropriate phenomenal representation of it. I refer to *non*-hallucinatory experience; but even hallucinations may have representational content. In my terminology, even if a hallucination of an object is so vivid as to be phenomenally indistinguishable from—and even qualitatively

---

the earth" (85). Whether he was committed to taking *propositional*, as opposed to attributive, belief to be entailed by perception in such cases is not clear.

identical with—perceiving it, it is only a *sensory* experience, not a perceptual one: there is nothing seen, heard, etc.[13]

### III. The Basis of Veridical Perception

Seeing three-dimensional objects is a good example for a reason not yet apparent. Let me, then, indicate some core elements of seeing such objects.

First, we never (directly) see *all* of an object such as a tree, animal, or building; we see only the part facing us. On the most intuitively plausible account, we see objects in virtue of seeing certain of their properties, such as (even if distortedly) their shape.[14] Second, no inference is required: seeing an object, including attributive seeing of it, is *constituted* by seeing the appropriate properties, for instance green and leafy; it is not a case of, or dependent on, inferring, from propositions about the object, that it is (say) green and leafy.

#### Phenomenal versus Physical Properties

Perceptual experience has long seemed to some philosophers to entail acquaintance with phenomenal properties as well as with

---

[13] For valuable discussion of perceptual representation different from, but in some ways supportive of, mine, see Justin P. McBrayer, "A Limited Defense of Moral Perception," *Philosophical Studies* 149, no. 3 (2010): 305–20. He plausibly replies to the charge that moral perception is not causal in "Moral Perception and the Causal Objection," *Ratio* 23, no. 3 (2010): 201–307.

[14] The most intuitive account of such seeing (an account which I take Bishop Berkeley, in his *Principles of Human Knowledge*, to have relied on for his phenomenalism) is that we see objects in virtue of seeing their properties. We can grant the perspectival character of seeing, however, without taking the object seen to be a construct out of the perceptually accessible properties.

certain of the physical properties of the perceived object. Consider viewing the rim of a drinking glass from an angle. In what we might call "uncorrected" visual experience, the rim will commonly appear to be elliptical. But, despite the look of the glass from this perspective, ellipticality is not a property of an ordinary drinking glass. Thus, talk of seeing the properties of objects must sometimes be understood in terms of properties that, in some appropriate way, represent the properties of the object seen but do not belong to it. There is of course a physical property of ellipticality, and we can understand how a phenomenally visual awareness of this property can, under the right conditions, indicate to the viewer the actual, incompatible shape of a round glass. What, then, is the phenomenal property that we instantiate when we see the glass *as* having an elliptical rim?[15] There is no elliptical object present, nor, on my view, any special object, such as a sense-datum, that can bear a phenomenal property of ellipticality or indeed any properties at all.

The positive view I propose is that the phenomenal property in question is what we might call *visually sensing elliptically*—visually sensing in an "elliptical manner," one might say, since we are speaking in terms of an adverb of manner (some speak similarly of *being visually appeared to elliptically*). This is an adverbially described common experience that we normally have in viewing a glass from a sharp angle. I take having that experience—experiencing in the relevant phenomenal way—to be a psychological property of the perceiver. This position does not entail that the viewer is acquainted with a sense-datum, an

---

[15] I refer to a *visual* appearance; we don't see—in the sense of 'regard'—the rim as elliptical in the *cognitive* sense implying we would attribute ellipticality to it.

object "given" to sense, that in fact is elliptical. The perceiver need not even be aware of the phenomenal property itself; instantiating that property makes possible a higher-order awareness of it, but does not require having that awareness.

By contrast, on the sense-datum view, there are phenomenal properties of these special, presumably mind-dependent, objects (sense-data)—objects that have their own properties, such as phenomenal ellipticality; and these properties in turn represent physical objects to perceivers. My view countenances no such objects as sense-data, and we need not posit acquaintance with a phenomenal property of ellipticality in order to explain the experience of seeming to see an elliptical rim. The phenomenal property in question—visually sensing elliptically—is a higher-order property of persons that they have by virtue of being sensorily aware of the property of ellipticality.[16] There are persons; there are physical properties; and there are sensory experiences in which we are aware of those properties. When, in perceiving an object, we are visually appeared to in a given way, we instantiate

---

[16] The position articulated here is a clarification of the one expressed in my "Moral Perception and Moral Knowledge," *Proceedings of the Aristotelian Society* 84 (2010): 79–97, which contains earlier versions of much that is in Chapters 1 and 2. A still earlier version of the position, which contrasts it with the sense-datum view, is expressed and defended in more detail in my *Epistemology*, chap. 2. I should add that the property is higher-order not because it is a property of a property but because the property of sensing elliptically conceptually "contains" a reference to the less complex, first-order property of being elliptical. My view does not imply that nothing is "given" in perception, but this is not the place to examine the "myth of the given." For recent discussions of that, see Mark Eli Kalderon, "Before the Law," *Philosophical Issues* 21 (2011): 219–44, and Martine Nida-Rumelin, "Phenomenal Presence and Perceptual Awareness: A Subjectivist Account of Perceptual Openness to the World," *Philosophical Issues* 21 (2011): 352–83.

a phenomenal property.[17] This experience may be just like one of seeing an elliptical rim; but that is not because we are acquainted with something that is elliptical. It is because something round appears to us in a way that evokes the visual sense of ellipticality. If we may be said to be aware of the property of ellipticality, it is not because we perceive or are acquainted with something—whether physical or a sense-datum—that has this property.

It seems to be an empirical question whether, if one has *never* seen an elliptical object, one might still have the awareness of ellipticality that goes with sensing elliptically. Arguably, the phenomenal (sensory) property would never occur in one's experience if one has never had a perceptual experience of something actually elliptical. I doubt this, but in any case the possibility of hallucination apparently shows that sensory awareness of ellipticality—a phenomenal as distinct from perceptual awareness of it—does not entail simultaneous awareness of any object possessing it.

The kind of awareness of properties so far considered—perceptual as opposed to intellective awareness—has a phenomenal element. Perceptual awareness of properties, moreover, may require that instances of them play a causal role in producing or sustaining that awareness; but if so, what of hallucinations? Since hallucinations can occur when the sense in question receives no external stimuli, as where someone who has lost eyesight visually hallucinates a loved one, an adequate account of sensory experience should avoid taking it to contain an external object that is in

---

[17] Not all phenomenal properties are sensory, even where that term extends to inner sense, as where inner sense yields a dull pain above the eyes. Imaging—seeing in the mind's eye—and inner speaking are also phenomenal.

some attenuated or abnormal way perceived. Here it is important to realize that what we are aware of can be abstract.

There appear, then, to be at least two kinds of awareness of properties, intellective and phenomenal. Suppose that, normally, the former requires—if only earlier in life—a route through the latter and in some cases may have a phenomenal element. It may still be true that non-physical awareness of a property, as in hallucination, can produce a visual or other sensory experience that seems to the subject just like seeing. The phenomenal awareness here can be phenomenally rich even if its object—a property—is abstract. Intellective awareness can also be rich, but is not my concern here. It is, however, important: on the epistemology I find most plausible, it is the conceptual kind of awareness that apparently underlies a priori knowledge.[18]

Suppose that we regard the objects of the most basic kind of perception as the sorts of physical properties by which we see spatiotemporal things. Those things themselves are plausibly taken to be seen by virtue of seeing their properties: the color and shape of a tree, the round, dark, treaded look of tires, the rising silvery shape of a plane in takeoff. How, then, can we maintain that perception is a causal relation to the object perceived? This object, after all, is what causes the perceptual experience; the cause is not something abstract, such as a property. The problem here is one for perception in general and must be solved if we are to understand moral perception.

---

[18] A sketch of the associated account of the a priori and references to alternative views is provided in my "Skepticism about the A Priori." For a related exploration of the epistemic role of visual experience in yielding a priori knowledge, see Marcus Giaquinto, *Visual Thinking in Mathematics* (Oxford: Oxford University Press, 2011).

### *The Causal Element Partly Constitutive*
### *of the Perceptual Relation*

For our purposes, it is best to approach the difficult question of how to characterize the terms of the relevant causal relations by first considering how to understand attributions of causation to substances. Consider saying that what caused a dent in a car's door was a stone, a paradigm of a substance. Surely we mean something like this: the event of the stone's hitting the door dented it, i.e., caused the event of its becoming dented (a distorting of its surface). The problem here for a causal theory of perception is to explain what causes perceptual experiences. Many perceptual experiences are not events, but ongoing impressions; nor need objects of perception, even in moral cases, be events. One could see an injustice by viewing the distribution of someone's grades for a set of students in a seminar one has fully attended (say, where the weakest two have very high grades while the strongest has a very low one).

A natural account of how substances figure in causing perceptual experiences arises from analysis of event causation and sustaining causation. My now seeing a hand is causally sustained by the hand's now having the observable property of being five-fingered, upraised, and so on for each of its properties that I see. With momentary perceptions, such as hearing a shot, the perceptual object's occurrence, a bang in this case (or a change, as where a rifle changes from being silent to banging), causes an event of, say, hearing a banging sound. Similarly, if I raise my hand before my eyes, that event causes my visual experience of its rising, which is a partly phenomenal event.

The metaphysical problem here is to explicate what kinds of objects are designated by the noun phrases naturally used in the relevant cases, for instance 'my hand's turning' and 'the flagpole's standing still'. We immediately encounter ambiguity: such phrases can designate types (properties) or tokens (concrete instantiations of properties). If I raise my hand twice, there are two tokens of the type, raising my hand. If the flagpole stands still after each gust of wind, there are as many tokens of that state property, the flagpole's standing still, as there are gusts. The type is abstract and hence the wrong kind of thing to be a cause. I call the event token a *dependent particular*. It is a particular because it is a unique thing in time and, at least for physical events, space; it is dependent because there must be an object that instantiates the property of turning (and, for at least event properties, *tokens* it). Ontologically, the hand is more basic than its turning: the hand can exist without its turning, but not conversely.

Connecting this ontological point about events with the causal theory of perception yields the view that what causes our perceiving a substance is its instantiating (tokening) some suitable set of properties, commonly including at least one observable property, such as its color or shape, or a sound it makes.[19] Unless the perception is strictly momentary, there will be both event causation and sustaining causation: even for my seeing my hand steadily, in which case my visual experience is sustained by the hand, there is an event of my *starting* to see it, followed by the state of my continuing to see it. That state is sustained by the tem-

[19] One might wonder how the causative property could fail to be observable; but the causative token need not be observable, as opposed to intimately connected with an observable property as, e.g., tokening light-ray reflection is intimately connected (but not identical) with having a color.

porally extended instantiations of the relevant properties of the hand, normally observable properties such as a color or shape. How this view of perception bears on moral cases will be shown in Chapter 2.

————

Let me draw together some main points about perception that have emerged, again speaking in terms of seeing as a paradigm. To see an object is to see some suitable subset of its properties.[20] Seeing these is a matter of an appropriate causal relation between its instantiating such properties and our phenomenal awareness of them: i.e., our instantiation of certain phenomenal properties—a kind of sensory representation—of the visible properties in question. This theory of perception is realist, mentalist, and (in the indicated sense) representationalist. There must be a real object perceived; perceiving it must be experiential in a sense entailing mentality; and the perceptual experience must in some way represent the object.

The realism may seem indirect, but it is as direct as a plausible realism can be. There is no more direct way to see a physical object than by seeing its properties. We could say that perception is "mediated" by awareness of properties, but this is misleading: the properties are not intermediary concrete objects, like sense-data, nor is one's perceptual sense of the object distinct from one's perceptual sense of its properties. The main concrete things posited—as opposed to properties, which are abstract entities—

[20] The property might be relational: I can see a distant plane when I misperceive its color and shape but I see its approximate location (a relational property) and its relation to me produces a suitable phenomenal responsiveness to changes in it, say a sense of its moving eastward when it does. I must here ignore these and other complications.

are the perceiver and the object perceived. The property instantiations by the perceiver and the object perceived are elements in the perceptual relation itself, and, ontologically, they are built from perceivers, universals, and perceptible particulars that instantiate those universals.

How well can the theory of perception just sketched accommodate moral perception, such as seeing injustice? This is the main question addressed in the next chapter. Of particular importance is to explain how the causal element in perception can be accommodated in the moral case, since moral properties are commonly conceived as normative and often taken to be outside the causal order. We must, then, consider not only how causation figures in moral perception but some central points about the nature of moral properties themselves.

# CHAPTER 2

# Moral Perception: Causal, Phenomenological, and Epistemological Elements

WE SHOULD BEGIN WITH CLARIFICATION of the problem to be addressed. What kind of experience might be thought to constitute moral perception?

## I. THE PERCEPTION OF RIGHT AND WRONG

Many philosophers think that moral knowledge is never perceptual and that perception is relevant to ethics only by representing certain non-moral facts. These are the kind that, like the fact that one person clubbed another, can be ascertained without applying or even having moral concepts. Responding to this skeptical view requires both an account of perception and an understanding of the basis on which singular moral judgments are made. Singular moral judgments are of the common kind in which a particular person or group of persons is said either (prospectively) to be obligated to do something, say by a promise, or (retrospectively) to have done the right thing (for instance by willing money to charities) or to have acted immorally, say by taking a bribe.

## Moral Perception versus Perception of the Moral

It is essential to distinguish between *moral perception* and mere *perception of a moral phenomenon*, for instance perception which is simply of a deed that has moral properties—something possible for a person who has no moral sensitivity or even moral concepts. Seeing a deed that has a moral property—for instance the property of being wrong—does not entail seeing its wrongness. We can see a theft, as where we see someone break a store window and seize jewelry. We can hear a lie, as where people tell us they telephoned us at a time we know we were listening in vain for a call. And of course we can feel a stabbing. These three cases, conceived minimally in terms of what is sensorily represented in experience, are perceptions of non-moral phenomena. They vary in what might be called directness, but they are all cases of perception. Can we, however, also perceive the moral wrongs that these acts commonly entail? As to the case of seeing the rightness of something—a property that is positive from the moral point of view—we may, in everyday language, say such things as that we are relieved to see justice done or gratified to see a long-evaded moral obligation at last fulfilled. But is justice itself, as exhibited by, say, equal treatment of citizens, ever genuinely perceptible?

This book argues for a positive answer. Further examples provide some support for that answer. We sometimes speak as if we have actually seen a moral property (or an instance of one). In answer to 'Did you ever see him wrong her?' one could properly say, 'Yes, I saw him spill hot tea on her hand when she was describing an incident that embarrassed him'. And could one not see terrible injustice by viewing soldiers shooting citizens who are peaceably criticizing their government?

If we are guided by how 'perceive' is used in English, we might go further still and say that there can be perception of certain traits of moral character. Some people seem visibly good. Someone might say, 'Just take a problem to her and in minutes you will see her goodness—it positively shines'. Doubtless such seeing of goodness comes by way of seeing manifestations of it. That is not how the moral rights and wrongs so far illustrated are seen, but perhaps there are two (or more) significantly different ways to see a moral property. Seeing her goodness is a kind of indirect seeing. Still, if the relevant manifestations of her character *bespeak* goodness—in reflecting it clearly and reliably—there appears to be a sense in which that goodness is indeed seen. We can see a plane in the distance by seeing a speck and hearing a distant roar. Might goodness not be sometimes manifested by comparably visible signs? Granted, whereas we see, for instance, the wrong in the theft by seeing its *ground*—the seizure of someone else's property—we see a person's goodness by seeing its *manifestations*. But this difference indicates two bases (and kinds) of moral perception; the difference is not (as will soon be argued) between an instance of seeing and one of inferring.

There is, then, some reason to take literally discourse that represents moral properties—or apparent moral properties—as perceptible. One objection to taking such discourse literally is that we do not see or in any sense perceive moral properties, but only non-moral properties or events that evidence their presence. Skeptics and noncognitivists may go further: they might say that at best we perceive natural properties that cause us to tend to ascribe moral properties (or apply moral predicates) to their possessors or to express moral judgments about those acts, persons, or other objects of moral appraisal. I grant that much of what I say about moral perception can be accommodated to a noncognitivist or other anti-realist view on which there are no moral properties but instead moral attitudes and moral language appropriate to them. In this book my response to this view and to skepticism is indirect: I simply aim to present a more plausible alternative.

Suppose the causal hypothesis just mentioned is true and that we do indeed tend to ascribe—and to say we see—moral properties because we perceive certain non-moral ones. We must still ask what relations hold between the two sorts of properties[1] and between non-moral judgments and moral judgments. Second, we must ask whether these relations differ importantly from relations common outside the moral realm. Third, if they do, does the difference show that we do not acquire moral knowledge or moral justification through perceptions of the kinds I have illustrated? Answering these questions (which will be pursued further in later chapters) requires establishing some basic points about moral perception.

To begin with, we should not expect moral perception to be exactly like physical perception, at least not exactly like perceiving everyday visible objects seen in normal light. First, moral properties are not easily conceived as observable, in what seems the most elementary way: no sensory phenomenal representation is possible for them, as opposed to intellective representations, though these may be integrated with phenomenal elements.[2] Second, even the perceptible properties on which the

---

[1] As suggested in the text, I assume here that there are moral properties. If my position in this book is plausible, that in itself provides reason to favor cognitivism in ethics. Perceptual beliefs are paradigms of cognition.

[2] Compare, however, Mark Wynn's characterization of "the perception of value." See esp. chap. 3 of *Emotional Experience and Religious Understanding*

possession of moral properties is often based may not be strictly speaking observable, at least in this elementary way. You can see Wang do an injustice to Xiaohui by, for example, witnessing his stealing jewelry from her handbag or his falsely accusing her of theft. But arguably, what is observable is Wang's removal of (say) a bracelet or his audible action of accusing her of theft. Still, you might count Wang's false accusation among the "observable facts"—because you see and hear the accusatory speech act and you know that the accusation is false. What we observe may be not just a matter of what we perceive; it may also depend on what we already know. We must grant, however, that even though you can visually observe the basis of the falsity, such as, rolled into an accuser's hand, the money the accused is said to have stolen, your seeing the injustice depends on your understanding the significance of the discrepancy between this visible fact and the content of the accusation.

## The Perceptual and the Perceptible

We should distinguish between two kinds of properties that, though their presence can be known by inference, are each capable of being objects of non-inferential acquaintance: the

---

(Cambridge: Cambridge University Press, 2005). He seems to agree with John McDowell that "we should think of values as 'in the world' … on McDowell's account, it is by way of our affective responses that we come to recognize these values" (9). The reference is to McDowell's "Non-Cognitivism and Rule-Following," in *Wittgenstein: To Follow a Rule*, ed. S. Holtzmann and C. Leich (London: Routledge and Kegan Paul, 1981). Cf. the passages Wynn quotes from Quentin Smith and Friedrich Schleiermacher (64 and 66). For more detailed discussion of the perceptibility of value, see Robert C. Roberts, *The Heart of the Virtues: Emotion's Role in the Moral Life*, forthcoming from Cambridge University Press.

*perceptual* and the *perceptible*. The former are sensory properties and include colors and shapes, textures and resonances, and other properties familiar in sense experience. There is no ordinary perception without them. The latter are not all sensory and include certain moral properties: being wrong, being unjust, and being obligatory, among others. Perceptual properties are perceptible, but not all perceptible properties are perceptual, nor need every *instance* of a perceptible property such as injustice be perceptible. A number of our examples indicate how perception reveals the perceptible. We can see this more clearly by considering whether the kind of perceptibility in question is a matter of being *observable*.

Is injustice observable, in the most basic sense, which apparently goes with perceptual properties? Is seeing injustice, for example, observational in the sense corresponding to perceptual properties? Or is such moral perception seeing—in a way that is at least not narrowly observational—a set of "base properties" for injustice, i.e., seeing properties on which injustice is consequential in a way that makes it obvious that an injustice is done? In asking this, I assume something widely held: that actions and other bearers of moral properties do not have those properties *brutely*, but on the *basis* of (consequentially on) having "descriptive" properties. An act is not simply wrong, in the way in which an act can be simply a moving of one's hand.[3] It is essential to the wrongness of an act that is wrong that it be wrong on the basis of

---

[3] I do not assume that there are any properties not grounded in others, but only that the way moral properties are grounded in descriptive ones is different from the way the property of intentionally moving one's hand is grounded in, say, intentional elements such as desires. Even if the difference is not one of modality, whether conceptual or ontic, there is an epistemic difference (clarified in the text) and that is the more important one for this book.

being a lie, or *because* it is a promise breaking, or *as* a stabbing, and so forth. Similarly, a person is not simply good, but good because of having good governing motives together with beliefs appropriate to guide one toward constructive ends.[4]

The question, then, is whether one ever really sees a moral phenomenon, such as an injustice. Recall the distinction between seeing an action that is wrong and seeing its wrongness. Clearly, one can see a deed that *is* wrong (unjust, a violation of a moral right, and so forth); this requires simply seeing the deed and its in fact being wrong. One can also see the deed *as* wrong; this requires seeing it and in some way viewing it as wrong. Third, we can see *that* a wrong is done; one way this is possible is by seeing that a deed is done and, partly on that basis, realizing, from seeing properties one knows it to have, that it is wrong. But, in any of these three cases, do we literally see such properties as wrongness or injustice? Consider seeing a colleague's writing a B on a student's report rather than an A, which, from our own careful reading, we know is deserved. Do we, in virtue of observing the falsification, see an injustice? Surely we may, but the moral perception this illustrates is not the elementary kind of perception illustrated by seeing the shape of a tree.

Does moral perception, however, differ in kind from every sort of non-moral perception? One might think that the phenomenal elements in perception properly so called must be sensory in the representational way that characterizes paradigms of seeing and

---

[4] That moral properties are consequential is a view elaborated in G. E. Moore's *Principia Ethica* (Cambridge: Cambridge University Press, 1903) and W. D. Ross's *The Right and the Good* (Oxford: Oxford University Press, 1930), reprinted in 2002, with an extensive introduction by Philip Stratton-Lake, by Hackett Pub. Co. (Indianapolis, IN, 1988), (esp. chap. 2). It is developed further in chap. 2 of *The Good in the Right*.

some of the other four ordinary senses. But why should we expect perception of injustice, which is a normative, non-sensory phenomenon, to be just like perception of color, shape, flavor, or sound, which are physical or in any case sensory and nonnormative? Why should there not be, for instance, a phenomenal sense of injustice that is—appropriately—not "pictorial" in the way exemplified by the visual impression of a tree or a painting? Where a moral perception is auditory, as with hearing a lie, or tactual, as with feeling a stabbing, we are not tempted to expect it to be pictorial, at least in the way visual experience may be taken to be. One might, however, still think that perceptual experience must be cartographic, embodying a "mapping" from phenomenal properties, such as a tactual impression of a shape or a visual impression of four squares in a painting, to properties of the object perceived, say division into four squares? I think not. What we see must be perceptible; but even if perceptible properties, such as being wrong or unjust, must be seen by seeing perceptual properties, such as bodily movements, the latter do not exhaust the former. The senses can yield the base by which we see certain perceptible properties without their being on the same level as the perceptual properties pictured or mapped by the senses.

If seeing physical objects dominates one's thinking about perception, pictorial and cartographic representation may seem to exhaust perception. The influence of seeing perceptual properties—those designated by narrowly observational terms—on philosophical accounts of perception is far-reaching. Hume, for example, conceived perception in terms of impressions. If one imagines impressing what one sees on wax—which can record visualized color and shape quite faithfully—one can see why perceptual representation might be conceived cartographically.[5] The colored wax impression is like a topographical map of what is seen. But perception is not mental mapmaking, and perceptual representation need not be cartographic. Even olfactory, gustatory, and perhaps auditory, perceptions indicate that point. Many such experiences are one-dimensional in a way that common visual experience is not—though seeing nothing but, for instance, the black wall of a ship from a rowboat by its side could be one-dimensional. Where there is no variation in a sensory field, there is normally nothing the sensory experience seems to map. Given these points, we can see that although, for certain cases of injustice, we can perhaps find, for the concrete deed seen to be unjust, a kind of mapping from the perceptual sense of injustice to certain of the *base* properties of injustice, there is no phenomenal property that has a cartographic representational relation to the property of injustice itself.

## II. The Representational Character of Moral Perception

In the light of what has emerged so far, we may distinguish two conceptions of moral perception. One centers on a phenomenal—and especially, a cartographic—representation of, say, injustice. The other, which is more plausible, centers on a phenomenal representation constituted by a (richer) perceptual *response* to injustice. The sense of injustice, then, a kind of impression of it, one might say, *as* based on, and as phenomenally integrated

---

[5] Cf. Locke's idea that the mind at birth is a "tabula rasa"—a blank tablet waiting for the hands of experience, especially perceptual experience, to inscribe on it the information experience supplies. Again, it is easy to see how a natural metaphor can cause one to tend to conceive perceptual representation cartographically.

with, a suitable ordinary perception of the properties on which injustice is consequential—*grounded*, to use another term for the same relation—might serve as the experiential element in moral perception.[6]

An important constituent in this phenomenal integration is the perceiver's felt sense of connection between, on the one hand, the impression of, say, injustice or (on the positive side) beneficence and, on the other hand, the properties that ground the moral phenomena. This felt sense of connection normally produces a non-inferential disposition to attribute the moral property of the action (or other phenomenon in question) on the basis of the property or set of properties (of that action) on which the moral property is grounded. Suppose, for instance, that I see injustice in a distribution. My sense of injustice normally yields a disposition to believe that distribution to be wrong *because* it is (on the ground that it is), say, giving more to one person than to another who is in the same needy position. My attribution of injustice, however, if perceptual, is non-inferential[7] and in any case need not be tied to the term 'injustice' or any synonym. Any of a range of terms may be appropriate, and we may indeed leave

---

[6] Compare Jonathan Dancy: "[T]hough we can discern reasons across the board, our ability to do it is not sensory; it is not sensibility that issues in the recognition of reasons (though sensibility may be required along the way); it is rather our capacity to judge . . . We might, I suppose, conceive judgement in general as a *response* to recognized reasons. . . .". See *Ethics without Principles* (Oxford: Clarendon Press, 2004), 144. This seems consistent with my view; and if recognizing reasons can be accomplished by discriminating base properties for a moral property central in a judgment, then if, as I hold, some cases of recognition are integrated with a certain phenomenology and an understanding of the relevant moral concepts, my view of moral perception (simple and propositional) accommodates the conception of certain (prima facie) moral judgments sketched here.

[7] More is said later in this and other chapters to explain why many moral attributions can be non-inferential.

open the extent to which the property attribution depends on the perceiver's use of language at all.

I take *moral* perception to carry a phenomenal sense—which may, but need not, be emotional—of the moral character of the act. This sense may, for instance, be felt disapproval, or even a kind of revulsion, as where we see a man deliberately spill hot tea on his wife's hand. It need not be highly specific; it may, for instance, be a felt *unfittingness* between the deed and the context, as where we see a male and female treated unequally in a distribution of bonuses for the same work. Positively, a felt fittingness may play a similar phenomenal role in moral perception. Think of the satisfying sense of moral restoration when one sees a person one cares about apologize to someone else one cares about after an offensive remark; the apology befits the offense. Moral perception is also possible where the object is one's own action, as where we suddenly see that we are being unfair to someone we are criticizing.[8]

In each instance, the moral sense of wrongness, injustice, or, in the positive case, welcome reparation is essentially connected to perception of non-moral properties on which the moral properties are grounded. In cases like these, we might be said to *sense morally*. This is not because moral properties are sensory—they are not—but because there is a kind of perceptual experience

---

[8] If perceptions are, as I suggest, experiential, it is natural to conceive moral perceptions as moral experiences. Self-perceptions may be included here, but of course not all self-perceptions of morally significant phenomena, such as acting from a sense of moral obligation, are moral perceptions, nor are moral perceptions the only kind of moral experience. In "The Axiology of Moral Experience" (*Journal of Ethics* 2 [1998]: 355–75) I have provided an account of moral experience that supports my theory of moral perception and my view (in Chapter 5) of the relation between the moral and aesthetic perception.

that appropriately incorporates the properties that ground the moral property that we sense. Perceptibility is not exhausted by perceptuality.

### Moral Properties and the Perception of Emotion

Here we can learn much by comparing moral perception with seeing an angry outburst that might evoke the comment 'I've never seen such anger!' Shall we say that the anger is not perceived because it is seen through seeing what might be called constitutive manifestations of it, such as redness of countenance, screaming, and heavy breathing? Granted, these can be mimicked by a good actor; but the facade of a house may similarly mimic a complete structure, concealing empty space behind what looks like the front wall of a large residence. We should not conclude that houses are never seen. Why, then, may some injustices not be as perceptible as anger?

It is true that whereas anger is seen by its manifestations, moral wrongs (and other phenomena) are seen by their grounds. But why should moral perception be conceived as limited to responses to effects rather than causes or grounds? More broadly, why should perception not be possible as a response to a variety of other reliable indicators or determinants of the perceived phenomenon? Suppose we think of perception as—in part—a kind of reception and processing of information by a causal path from an information source to the mind, where the processing need not imply events in consciousness.[9] This conception cer-

---

[9] For discussion of the sense in which perception is information processing, Fred Dretske's *Knowledge and the Flow of Information* (Cambridge, MA: MIT

tainly comports well with the role perception plays in providing empirical knowledge. On this conception, it should not matter whether the information impinging on the senses is determined by what is perceived or, instead, determines or evidences that. We can know a thing either by its effects that mark its presence or by its causes that guarantee its occurrence.

Consider the latter kind of case—perception by grounds— through an example of perception that yields perceptual knowledge that arises from seeing a causal ground. May I not report that I saw a killing if what I saw is one person put what I know is a fatal dose of a poison for which there is no antidote into another's whiskey, which the latter then fully drinks before my eyes? I see an act that *is* a killing and, given my background knowledge, see it to be one. If the passage of time makes it seem that the action of killing is not complete until the death, note that the relationship between the causal information and the deed is the same as where one sees a powerful bomb explode next to a soldier but, owing to instantaneous smoke, does not see the inevitable resulting death. Has one not seen the killing? Seeing it need no more require seeing its typical indications or its entire temporal extent than seeing a house requires seeing all its windows and doors or its entire spatial extent.

Even if one insists that the killing cannot be properly said to have been seen until death occurs, the relation between that by which it is seen and the seeing of it is the same: the seen determinants are that by which the action, and the wrong it entails, are seen. The use of language I illustrate here is at least as old

Press, 1981) is a good source. Processing information is more than its mere reception; see Burge, *Origins of Objectivity*, e.g. 299–301, for discussion of both notions and points concerning Dretske's view.

as Shakespeare. In *Romeo and Juliet*, Mercutio, fatally stabbed, says, "I am sped" (act 3, scene 2); and in *Hamlet*, Laertes, fatally wounded by his own poisoned sword, confesses, "I am justly killed with mine own treachery" and continues with an affirmation that Hamlet too has been killed:

> . . . Hamlet, thou art slain;
> No medicine in the world can do thee good.
>
> (act 5, scene 2)

To be sure, the relation between the grounds of wrongdoing and the wrongdoing seen by them is not causal. The fatal poisoning does not cause the wrongdoing; it entails, in a way that implies partial constitution, the wrongdoing. But, as Laertes's wrongdoing illustrates, the relation is highly reliable. It can even be a necessary relation and so, from the point of view of perception as a kind of receiving of information, perfectly suitable to ground perception and indeed knowledge.

It must also be granted that whereas someone perceptually normal cannot ordinarily view a tree in daylight without the usual arboreal representational experience, many people *can* view a perceptible injustice without perceiving injustice or having any moral phenomenal response, such as an intuitive sense of wrongdoing. But the proportion of people who are morally percipient, or indeed morally normal at all, is smaller than the proportion who are perceptually normal. Moreover, injustice can be subtle, and the difficulty of perceiving it may, for some morally normal people, trace to the need for greater moral sensitivity than goes with mere moral normality. Compare seeing an injustice with seeing a painting in which a small figure of a person is sketched visibly but is not sharply distinct from background shrubbery. Someone who is perceptually normal but not an experienced viewer of paintings might not, without careful scrutiny or guidance, have any phenomenal response representing that figure. This does not imply that the figure is visually imperceptible. Similarly, a person's lacking a sense of injustice upon witnessing a visibly unjust deed does not imply that its injustice is morally imperceptible—certainly not to other observers. Insensitivity to a property does not imply its imperceptibility.[10]

It should be apparent, then, that the theory of perception I have outlined can accommodate moral perception by incorporating a distinction between perceptual representations of an ordinary sensory kind and perceptual representations that are of a richer kind and have a moral element. Can this broad theory of perception, however, explain how moral perception can have a causal character? It can. It does not do so by treating (moral) perceptual property instances like seeing injustice as causally produced or sustained by instances of moral properties. The theory is neutral regarding the possibility that moral properties themselves are causal. It does, however, construe seeing certain subsets of base properties for injustice as—at least given appropriate understanding of their connection to moral properties—a kind of perception of a moral property; and this kind includes, as elements, such ordinary perceptions as seeing a violent seizure of an old man's wallet and hearing an abusive vulgarity screamed at a conference speaker. Depending on our psycho-

---

[10] The view proposed is consistent with my ethical intuitionism developed in *The Good in the Right* and elsewhere; and this paragraph indicates how to meet an objection by Sarah McGrath to the idea that there is intuitive knowledge (not all of which, to be sure, is perceptual) of particular moral facts. See her "Moral Knowledge by Perception," *Philosophical Perspectives* 18 (2004): 209–29, esp. 223.

logical constitution, we may be unable to witness these things without a phenomenal sense of wrongdoing integrated with our perceptual representation of the wrong-making facts.[11] For many people, certain perceptible wrongs perpetrated in their presence are unignorable and moral perceptions of certain salient moral wrongs are virtually irresistible.

### Is Moral Perception Necessarily Conceptual?

We have seen the difference between a moral perception of wrongdoing and a perception that is merely of an act that *is* wrong. We have also seen that moral perception does not entail the formation of moral belief or judgment. Still, although moral perception is not belief-entailing, it remains true that given how we see certain base properties that are sufficient for injustice, we sometimes perceptually know, and are perceptually warranted in believing, that, for instance, one person is doing an injustice to another. We are thus warranted in seeing the deed *as* an injustice. When we have such perceptual knowledge or perceptual warrant, we are often properly describable as *seeing that* the first is doing an injustice to the second and, indeed, as knowing this.

This point does not imply that seeing *an injustice* is intrinsically conceptual. But seeing *that* an injustice is done *is* conceptual. A child who has yet to develop the concept of injustice can see an act that constitutes an injustice. A decade later, of course, the same perception might immediately yield a moral conceptu-

---

[11] For related work developing a partial phenomenology of moral perception, see Terry Horgan and Mark Timmons, "What Does Phenomenology Tell Us about Moral Objectivity?" *Social Theory and Policy* (2008): 267–300. They also explore phenomenological aspects of fittingness.

alization of the act or indeed moral knowledge thereof. Between these two points, the child may be disturbed at seeing an injustice in the kind of act in question, say giving a visibly much nicer pair of shoes to a twin sibling of the same sex taken to the same store just before the beginning of the school year. Prior to conceptualization, the child may have a sense of unfittingness in such action: the disparity in treatment disturbs the child who sees the sibling treated better. That perception of disparity, together with the sense of its unfittingness, reflects a discriminative sensitivity to differential treatment and puts the child in a good position to develop the concept of injustice. If this picture is correct, moral perception may precede, and indeed may be a normal developmental route to, moral concept-formation.

My view does not imply that *all* non-inferential moral knowledge of perceptible moral facts is itself perceptual. One might know such facts from memory or testimony. Those are non-inferential ways of knowing.[12] Conceivably, there could even be a subliminal detection capacity by which someone non-inferentially knows some such facts more directly. This kind of knowledge would be analogous to the sort possible through a kind of "blindsight."

By contrast, an experience constituting a moral perception must have a phenomenal element. Many elements of this kind might be called *perceptual moral seemings*. These are not equivalent to *intuitive moral seemings*, though they may produce those. Nor need a proposition known by moral perception be itself *intuitive*, in roughly the sense that we find it plausible upon considering it even in isolation from perceptual or other evidence for it.

---

[12] Why these kinds of knowledge should be considered non-inferential is explained in some detail in chaps. 3 and 7 of my *Epistemology*.

It may well be, however, that some perceptual moral seemings are related to intuitive seemings based on a hypothetical version of the same case, much as perceptual physical seemings, as
with ordinary vision, are related to an imaginational seeing of the
same object in the mind's eye. Even just picturing someone's giving different grades for equally good performances, as where we
recall seeing it, can produce an intuition of injustice, much as imaging one's viewing a glass from an angle can produce an (imaginational) impression of ellipticality. Recollective imagination can
*replay* perception; prospective imagination can *preplay* perception; and creative imagination can reach beyond perception both
in the variety of properties imagined and in their combinations.
Responsiveness to property instantiations is crucial in both cases.

Nothing said here implies that what perceptually seems to have
a property actually has it, nor need every perceptual or intuitive
seeming regarding a proposition—a (conscious) perceptual or
intuitive impression that it is true—yield belief of the proposition
it supports. A perceptually knowable proposition may be only a
*potential* object of a perceptual or an intuitive seeming, as where
someone sees a wrong and considers the nature of the deed but
does not initially have a sense that it is wrong or, especially, see
*that* it is wrong. Here seeing a wrong may not even be a moral
perception and certainly need not yield a propositional perception that the deed is wrong. We might see one man we view as
domineering shake the hand of another, smaller man of lower
rank before a meeting and notice a hard squeeze, with the result
of redness in the other's hand. It might not seem to us until later
that we have witnessed an intimidation, though we could have
been more alert and seen at the time that the former was wrongfully intimidating the latter. Moral perceptual seemings, more-

over, may or may not be partly emotional, as where indignation figures in them.[13]

It should be evident that my theory of moral perception is realist in taking moral properties to be genuine properties of actions and persons. But the theory also stresses phenomenal, attitudinal, and even emotional aspects of moral perception. With these kinds of psychological elements in mind, some philosophers have developed an extensive analogy between moral properties and secondary qualities or indeed treated the former as a subcase of the latter. This issue is too complicated to pursue here in depth.[14] It is appropriate, however, to indicate why my position is not fruitfully considered a secondary quality view. First, it is characteristic of such a view to take secondary qualities, for instance colors, to be not intrinsic properties of their possessors—not "in" the object that has them, as Locke put it—but dispositions on the

[13] Here and in many other places it will be evident that I am taking moral perceptions to arouse or have some other important connection with motivation and behavioral tendencies. My view can take account of many points about perception made by Alva Nöe in his wide-ranging *Action in Perception* (Cambridge, MA: MIT Press, 2004), but I do not accept all the elements in his "enactive" theory of perception, e.g. that "for perceptual sensation to constitute experience—that is, for it to have genuine representational content—the perceiver must possess and make use of *sensorimotor knowledge*" (17). Perhaps, however, this requirement is less stringent than one might think: a page earlier he says, "The enactive view insists that mere feeling is not sufficient for perceptual experience (i.e., for experience with world-representing content)" (16). I agree that it is insufficient; and for me the 'i.e.' suggests that in determining what counts as perception, kind of content may be more important than the sensorimotor condition and may at least qualify what that condition requires.

[14] For a detailed critical discussion of the secondary quality view, see Elizabeth Tropman, "Intuitionism and the Secondary Quality Analogy in Ethics," *Journal of Value Inquiry* 44 (2010): 31–45. For a contrasting sympathetic presentation of the analogy, see Justin D'Arms and Daniel Jacobson, "Sensibility Theory and Projectivism," in *The Oxford Handbook of Ethical Theory*, ed. David Copp (Oxford: Oxford University Press, 2006), 186–218.

part of the object to produce certain phenomenal properties in the observer. On my view, moral properties do belong to, and are in that sense "in," their objects. They do entail that competent observers of these objects *tend* to have a certain kind of experience, but they are not constituted by this tendency. Second, whereas the secondary quality theorists tend to think that the nature of moral properties depends on human responses in the way color properties apparently do, I deny this. Certainly a morally sound observer of, say, brutal injustice will tend to have a disapproving experience; but surely there could be such moral properties (and acts exhibiting them) even if there were no morally sound observers but only barbarous offenders.

———

On the view of perception presented in Chapter 1, perception is a kind of experiential information-bearing relation between the perceiver and the object perceived. I have not offered a full analysis of this relation but have said enough to indicate how, even if moral properties are not themselves causal, they can be perceptible. We perceive them by perceiving properties that ground them, which, in turn, may or may not be perceived in the basic way in which we perceive some properties other than by perceiving still others. But the dependence of moral perception on non-moral perception does not imply an inferential dependence of all moral belief or moral judgment on non-moral belief or judgment (a point that, in Chapter 5, will also be illustrated in the aesthetic domain). Indeed, although perceiving moral properties, as where we see an injustice, commonly evokes belief, it need not. When it does, it may do so in a way that grounds that belief in perception of the properties of the unjust act in virtue of which it *is* unjust.

This kind of grounding explains how a moral belief arising in perception can constitute perceptual knowledge and can do so on grounds that are publicly accessible and, though not a guarantee of it, a basis for ethical agreement. There is more to be said about how this is possible and about how perceptual moral knowledge is connected not only with other moral knowledge but also with intuition and emotion, which, as later chapters will show, are significantly related to perception and perceptual knowledge.

CHAPTER 3

# *Perception as a Direct Source of Moral Knowledge*

SIMPLE PERCEPTION, WHETHER MORAL OR NOT, does not entail belief formation, but its non-doxastic character does not in the least preclude its presenting perceivers with much information about the object perceived. That perception does this explains in good part why it can both justify beliefs appropriately connected with its content and ground knowledge about its object. But if, in perceiving an object, we in some way process information—as is widely held among psychologists as well as philosophers—one may wonder whether perception is in some way inferential. Understanding perception requires pursuing this question, and that in turn requires clarifying what constitutes inference. This chapter explores how perception and inference differ and how each may yield moral knowledge.

## I. PERCEPTION AND INFERENCE

Some philosophers might contend that although we can see that (say) someone is writing 'He did only two hours of work', we can-

not see that an injustice was thereby done even when we know
he worked much longer. Rather, they might claim, from what we
visually know and background propositions we already believe,
we *infer* that an injustice was done. I grant that making such inferences is possible and also that the phrase 'see that' can designate inferential cognitions, as where 'see' means 'realize' and
what is realized comes via premises. Such cases often represent
inferential knowledge which rests on a premise yielded by perception. My point is that for some moral knowledge, we need
not posit an inference, as opposed to belief-formation that is a
direct response to a recognized pattern. An inference, as a tokening of an argument, is a mental event or process that requires
a set of premises and a conclusion. Inference is not needed for
responses to patterns, nor even for certain kinds of interpretation
of patterns or other complex phenomena. Think of the kind of
momentary outburst characteristic of breaking a fingernail when
one is trying to open a battery compartment. Someone observing
the incident may instantly interpret the outburst as frustration
rather than anger.[1]

Examples alone will not settle this matter. The relation between inference and moral perception deserves further exploration. Suppose we do posit an inference underlying the kind of
moral knowledge that is, on my view, perceptual. We must then
treat as inferential all our perceptual beliefs except the most elementary. We could not be properly said to see that someone is
angry or even that water is coming from a tap. The properties

---

[1] *The Good in the Right* addresses the role of inference in moral epistemology; and in *Practical Reasoning and Ethical Decision* (London: Routledge,
2006), esp. chaps. 4–6, I provide an account of the nature of inference and its
relation to belief formation.

that are observable in the narrow sense that goes with perceiving these phenomena do not discriminate between anger and a theatrical imitation of it or between water and ethyl alcohol. Making this discrimination is important if we need to *show* that we are seeing anger or water; but we must not impose the requirements for showing something on simply knowing it.[2] Moreover, positing inferences is not needed to account for how perceiving a pattern can mediate between perceptions of the elements in it and a belief the pattern produces. Compare facial recognition. We believe that someone approaching is (say) Karl because of the facial pattern we see, but seeing that is a matter of seeing many features of his face, not of drawing on myriad tacit premises attributing them.

Granted, facial recognition depends on *seeing* the features of the face, as is evidenced by the impossibility of recognition where a number of features are blocked, say the eyebrows. But such recognition is not dependent on *inference* from the relevant features, as is evidenced by the possibility of recognition even where the perceiver has no belief corresponding to those features. I need not believe Karl's brows have the look they do until I focus on the matter. Indeed, the look they have that is important for my recognition may be so distinctive—or so subtly related to other features, such as the nose and hairline—that it would be difficult, or perhaps impossible, to capture in the content of beliefs of propositions or, correspondingly, in a set of premises for inference.

Even if propositional moral perceptions, such as seeing that one person unjustly accused another, were in some sense inferential, attributive moral perceptions need not be. Just as, when

---

[2] This is argued in detail in *Epistemology*, esp. chaps. 13–14.

we glimpse copious cones hanging from its branches, we can see a spruce to be a conifer without inferring that it is a conifer from facts about it, we can see an act to be a wrong from properties of it, without inferring that it is wrong. Moral perceptions are similar in this respect. In seeing one person wrongfully intimidate another, we may have a phenomenal sense of the first wronging the second but only on reflection form a *belief* in which the concept of wrongness (or any moral concept) figures, say a belief that the first did a wrong toward the second, or that the act was unfair (unwarranted, immoral, or the like).[3]

Similarly, imagine hearing a judge issuing a sentence. We may have a sense of its unfittingness to the crime even prior to our forming—or without our forming—a belief, on that basis, that the sentence is unjust. To be sure, the phenomenal representation of voicing and diction may be psychologically so much more prominent than the moral sense of injustice that the latter is difficult to isolate and easy to miss, especially where it is not heightened by emotion. But the visual sensations representing a sad face may be similarly subtle. They may still be a basis for a perceptual belief about the person's mood, whether or not emotion figures in the perceiver's phenomenal response. Our responses to persons and their deeds, like our responses to paintings and sonatas, may be very finely adjusted to myriad perceptible prop-

---

[3] The point that seeing something to have a property does not entail a propositional belief that it has that property is still more plausible given that (as suggested in Chapter 1) seeing a thing to have a property does not even require *believing* it to have that property and thereby conceptualizing it as, say, a spruce; it apparently requires only a non-doxastic kind of discrimination of the property, whereas believing that a thing has the property requires conceptualizing the property.

erties without our drawing a single inference. Those responses may be moral, aesthetic, recognitional, or of some other character; and the complexity of their basis yields grounds for much genuine knowledge.

## II. Can Moral Perception Be Naturalized?

One might think that accounting for moral perception requires naturalizing moral properties so that they can figure in the causal order as do the observable properties familiar in much ordinary perception and in the natural sciences. I am not seeking to naturalize moral properties, nor does explaining the data we have considered in describing moral perception require such naturalization.[4] At least three points are needed here. First, the experiential responses to moral properties that entitle us to speak of moral perception are causally explainable in terms of their basis in the natural properties on which moral properties are consequential. Second, these responses can have this same basis whether or not moral properties are themselves causal. My account thus allows, though it does not require, a naturalizing of moral properties by providing a causal account of their constitution. Third, the question whether moral perception—or any other kind—can

---

[4] For critical discussion of Nicholas Sturgeon's "Cornell Realist" attempt to naturalize moral properties, originally presented in "Moral Explanations," in *Morality, Reason, and Truth*, ed. David Copp and David Zimmerman (Totowa, NJ: Rowman and Allanheld, 1985), see my "Ethical Naturalism and the Explanatory Power of Moral Concepts," in *Naturalism: A Critical Appraisal*, ed. Steven Wagner and Richard Warner (Notre Dame, IN: University of Notre Dame Press, 1993), 95–115. That paper argues that naturalizing moral explanations is possible without naturalizing moral properties and that some of the work those explanations do is non-causal.

be somehow inferential is orthogonal to the question whether only natural properties are perceptible: whether perception is inferential does not depend on whether its only direct objects are natural phenomena.

In *one* way, however, I am (non-reductively) naturalizing moral perception. For I not only take moral perception to be a causal relation but also grant that the base properties that ground moral properties are natural properties and have causal power if any properties do. Moral perception is a phenomenon that occurs in the natural, causal order. Moreover, the non-causal element important for understanding moral perception and knowledge acquired through moral perception does not require positing any supernatural being or even a Cartesian conception of the human person. That non-causal element is crucial for conceptual capacities that go with an adequate understanding of moral concepts and with the a priori character of the relation between moral properties and the non-moral, natural ones on which moral properties are consequential. The experience in virtue of which (in part) a moral perception counts as a perception is causally grounded in perception of natural properties, and the experience may be considered a causally grounded response to (though not merely an effect of) a moral property that is itself consequential on those natural properties. This holds even if the phenomenal element in that response is not pictorial, cartographic, or otherwise narrowly representational.[5]

---

[5] Space does not permit comparing this view with moral sense theories, but I take those to be best understood as naturalizing moral properties and making them response-dependent; I do neither. For a version of this view usefully contrasting with mine, see Michael Smith, "Objectivity and Moral Realism: On the Significance of the Phenomenology of Moral Experience," in Michael Smith, *Ethics and the A Priori* (Cambridge: Cambridge University Press, 2004).

My conclusion at this point, then, is this. Although moral properties are apparently not natural properties, they are constitutively anchored in natural properties, in an intimate way such that seeing or otherwise perceiving the natural properties or relations that are their base suffices, given an appropriate phenomenal response, to make it reasonable to describe certain experiences as perceptions of such moral properties as injustice and, more generally, wrongdoing.[6] Perceiving those base properties is perception of something that partly constitutes the perceptible moral property in question.[7] It is to be expected, then, that when moral perceptions like these occur, whether they are simple or attributive perceptions, the perceiver is in a position to see that something, such as an action or person, has the property in question. Such propositional perception embodies a kind of moral knowledge.

---

A related theory developed more closely in relation to empirical psychology is the "construct sentimentalism" of Jesse Prinz in *The Emotional Construction of Morals* (Oxford: Oxford University Press, 2007), which is examined in "Prinz's Subjectivist Moral Realism," a detailed critique by David Copp (*Nous* 45, no. 3 [2011]: 577–94). An informative discussion of sensibility accounts of moral judgments, with an examination of an anti-realist version, is provided by D'Arms and Jacobson, "Sensibility Theory and Projectivism."

[6] Readers who notice that most of my examples of moral perception are of wrongs rather than "rights" may wonder why. Arguably, the institution of morality is more strongly oriented toward preventing wrongs than toward producing right actions. It is also arguable that our being more sensitive to what violates obligations than to their fulfillments has fitness value. Pursuing these important (and compatible) hypotheses is beyond the scope of this book.

[7] I am not taking a constitution relation to be an identity relation; hence, even if being morally obligated to A is equivalent to (say) the proposition that A-ing is a promise keeping, a truth telling, a rendering of aid, or . . . the property of obligatoriness is simply that disjunctive property (if there are disjunctive properties). But there is surely a sense in which a particular act, such as wronging a friend by lying, is at least partly constituted by that lie.

## III. Moral Perception as a Basis
## of Moral Knowledge

Some of my examples bring out that moral perception always comes by way of non-moral perception. The relation here is not causal or instrumental, but rather *constitutive*. Moral perception is partly constituted by a certain kind of response to perceiving, for instance seeing, a moral phenomenon, such as an act constituting a kind of wrongdoing. Moral perception is not, properly speaking, caused by that seeing or by some other perception of a moral phenomenon; it *is* perceiving that phenomenon, in the moral way I have described. Compare seeing a smile by seeing the distinctively happy countenance that we call a smile. Where this is a comprehending perception such as occurs with normal attentive adults, and not a quasi-photographic representation of the face such as a dog might have, it is a way of seeing the facial expression in question. Moreover, just as it is by being a stabbing of a helpless old man that the deed seen (at least partly) constitutes a wrongdoing, when we smile by exhibiting the relevant facial expression, the 'by' here indicates a constitution relation: in the context, producing the happiness of countenance *is* smiling. It is not an ordinary means to smiling.[8]

### Basic and Non-basic Perception

If we reflect on cases like facial recognition, in which we acquire perceptual knowledge *by* perceiving other properties (though

---

[8] Note that when *x* is a constitutive as opposed to instrumental means to *y*, *y* is not possible without *x*. Smiling is not possible without the facial movements that constitute it, but telling a joke may or may not be a means to producing smiles. To be sure, the constitutive means can have more than one cause, as can smiling itself; an artificial smile, caused by stimulating the facial muscles through brain manipulation, is still a smile. But the relation between the constitutive means and what it constitutes is not contingent.

non-inferentially), we can distinguish between *basic* and *non-basic perception*. Perception of the shape and color properties of Karl's face is basic relative to perception of the property of being—as we might put it—"Karl-faced," but we do not normally infer that the face is Karl's from ascriptions of the more basic properties. With moral perception, the relation of the base properties—those on which moral properties are consequential—to the moral properties grounded on them is at least as intimate as that of facially constitutive properties to that of having the face in question. It is *more* intimate than the relation of anger-expressive properties to being angry. I see no good reason not to speak of moral perception if we can speak of facial perception and perception of anger. Perception is multileveled. Some kinds are more basic than others; and even if there happens to be a level that is ultimately basic for us as we are now constituted, the *concept* of perception does not dictate any final level, such as that of perceiving colors and shapes.[9]

[9] Note that I say, "if there happens to be a level that is basic for us"; I leave open that there is none, though in any given case of perception there cannot be an infinity of levels and so there must be a level basic *on that occasion*. This indicates my response to Jonathan Dancy, who, reacting to my point that moral properties are not observable in the sense that they are phenomenally representable, expressed doubt that "there is something elementary in all perception, so that, for instance, the mechanic's basic awareness cannot be of the defective functioning of the water pump." See "Moral Perception," *Proceedings of the Aristotelian Society*, supplementary volume, 84 (2010): 111 (this is a commentary on my "Moral Perception and Moral Knowledge"). I agree that a mechanic can simply hear the defectiveness of a water pump. But I doubt this is a basic perception. The mechanic surely hears the defectiveness in the way one normally recognizes a face—not by drawing an inference from an ascription of some telltale property but by responding to, say, a scraping at a certain pitch and loudness, an origin near the radiator, a contrast with the normal sounds, and so forth. Granted, we *could* evolve so that certain complex patterns are not in this way "decomposable"—perhaps some are not. This is a contingent matter on which my theory of perception is neutral.

Regarding the epistemology of moral perception generally, I have argued that there is a kind of experience properly called moral perception and that it can ground a certain kind of moral knowledge. Even apart from skepticism (which I here assume is avoidable), we should ask whether the grounding of the moral-perceptual beliefs in question is sufficiently reliable to qualify them as knowledge.

It must be granted that if we do not have good grounds for believing that the base properties are present (those on which a moral property is consequential), then we do not have good grounds for ascribing the moral property in question. This kind of dependency, however, is not peculiar to moral beliefs. If we lack grounds for believing that Wang is (say) red-faced and screaming as he hears of his son's wrecking the family car, we also lack good grounds for believing, on the basis of those indications, that he is angry. But notice this: although his having these properties is excellent evidence that he is angry, it does not *entail* this, whereas A's knowingly hiding the money that A is falsely accusing B of stealing does (non-formally) entail that A is (prima facie) wronging B. In the first case, the grounding relation is empirical and contingent; in the second, it is a priori and necessary.[10] Moreover, although in the first case we perceive a fact by what *it determines* and, in the second, by what *determines it*, in both cases the perceptual knowledge is reliably grounded and is so in part by virtue of a causal relation. In the moral case that relation is between properties that entail the in-

---

[10] That the relation between the base properties and the moral ones consequential on them is necessary and a priori is argued in chaps. 1 and 2 of *The Good in the Right* and "Skepticism about the A Priori," but the main points in this book do not depend on that strong view.

stantiation of the moral property in question and the perceiver's moral awareness of that property.

Consider a different example of evidential dependence. If we lack good grounds for believing that the lights have come back on, we also lack good grounds to believe, on the basis of this fact, that electricity is again flowing. But notice this: whereas the lights' being on is excellent evidence that the electricity is flowing, it does not entail that proposition, yet if a man really is knowingly hiding, behind his back, the money he is falsely accusing someone else of stealing, it does follow that he is wronging the other. As with the anger example, in the former case the grounding relation is empirical and contingent; in the latter it is a priori and necessary.

### Epistemic versus Inferential Dependence

My position, then, is that moral cognitions, such as moral judgments, can constitute perceptual knowledge but depend epistemically, though not inferentially, on non-moral elements. Take inferential dependence first. Suppose we know or justifiedly believe that a student plagiarized. This is typically because we know or justifiedly believe that, for instance, the student's paper is copied from the Internet (this would illustrate both epistemic and inferential dependence). Our knowledge is premise-based. Suppose, however, that we see a man slap his wife's face upon her asking him not to have another whiskey before driving home. If, as would be normal, we not only see the wrongdoing but also know *perceptually* that he wronged her, we know this non-inferentially, on the basis of our adequate perceptual grounds. Our need for this perceptual basis manifests an epistemic dependence, but not an inferential, premise-dependence. Our grounds are perceptual, not propositional.

Granted, inferential processing comes in many forms. Two people could play a game in which they slap each other after various insults meant to be simply witty. Suppose I know this game is being played at a party. Then my seeing a husband's slapping his wife might not lead me to believe he has wronged her, or might do so only after I form the belief—perhaps without articulating it to myself—that the wife's remark about driving after drinking was not part of the game. It should also be granted that it may be difficult to tell whether a belief is or is not inferential. But the difficulty of drawing a distinction in some cases does not imply that it is not quite clear in many others.

Our justification in my slapping example, like our knowledge in that same case, is also perceptual. We see the man slap his wife and, as with facial recognition, believe, on that visual basis and non-inferentially, that he wronged her. Our justification for this perceptual belief is as strong as the justification we would have for believing this non-perceptually, on the basis of premises ascribing to him the properties on which his wronging her is consequential, properties whose instantiation we have perceived. The strength of our justification is a matter of how well-grounded it is, not of the form in which the grounds are possessed: specifically, whether they are possessed in the form of perceptually received information or in the form of beliefs whose propositional objects express the same relevant information. The non-inferential belief that the tipsy husband wronged his wife can count as perceptual knowledge because of the way it is based on a phenomenal responsiveness to the moral property. That responsiveness, in turn, is causally grounded in perception of certain of the natural properties on which the moral property is consequential.

## Phenomenological Reliabilism

The position on perceptual moral knowledge defended here might be called a *phenomenological reliabilism*. It enables us to ground the possibility of a major kind of ethical objectivity. It accounts for the availability of intersubjectively accessible grounds for a wide range of moral judgments.[11] It also explains how some moral knowledge can meet strong reliabilist constraints, that is, how perceptual beliefs constituting moral knowledge are based on perceptions that, in the circumstances, guarantee the truth of the beliefs or make them very highly probable.

Perceptual moral justification meets constraints similar to but weaker than those applying to moral knowledge. Perceptual justification for believing that, for instance, an interviewer is wrongly intimidating the interviewee does not require quite as good a sense of the normative significance of the behavior that supports this judgment or as good evidence for wrongdoing. One might also be perceptually justified in such a case even if mistaken, whereas knowledge of a proposition implies its truth.

Explaining how certain moral beliefs and the corresponding moral judgments can meet strong reliabilist constraints is important. It paves the way for countenancing moral perception and the perceptual knowledge it can yield. My position does not imply, however, the even stronger conclusion that all non-perceptual moral knowledge rests on a foundation of perceptual moral knowledge, or even that we could not have the former without the latter. The account is consistent with the plausible view that,

---

[11] My reliabilism here concerns conditions for knowledge, not perception: it leaves open whether we can perceive something only given a "reliable" connection between its having, in the circumstances, the relevant properties and our perceptually responding to it (though this connection cannot be, in a certain way, accidental).

without our having some perceptual moral knowledge, we would have no moral knowledge; but it leaves open the possibility that even apart from moral perception, we could have both inferential and non-inferential moral knowledge of, and justification for, moral judgments. The account does not foreclose the possibility that moral concepts are acquired through a combination of non-moral perception and moral concept-formation.[12]

Developmentally, these two cognitive elements in nomal human lives—non-moral perception and moral concept-formation—yield an understanding of the notions of right and wrong, of the obligatory and the permissible, and of other normative concepts. I have stressed that moral perception naturally occurs in this developmental process, but I have left room for other developmental views. A certain kind of Platonism might posit development of moral concepts by rational insight into the abstract and might explain singular moral knowledge by appeal to subsumption of particulars under moral concepts. This subsumptivist view is not required by a Platonistic theory of general moral concepts, but it might be developed compatibly with that view as naturally as (with qualifications) the contrasting position I have presented. On my view, even if we regard moral concepts as abstract entities,

---

[12] This paragraph indicates some of the reasons why my theory of moral perception should not be conceived as a "perceptual account of moral knowledge" in general, as seems to be suggested by Carla Bagnoli in "Moral Perception and Knowledge by Principles," in *The New Intuitionism*, ed. Jill Graper Hernandez (London: Continuum, 2011), 101–3. Knowledge of moral principles and subsumptive knowledge of singular moral propositions are not perceptual, though at least the latter may epistemically depend on perception. It is an interesting question whether, for classical utilitarianism, there can be perceptual moral knowledge. Consider wrongness. This is suboptimality with respect to consequences for hedonic (or other non-moral) consequences. It is not clear how this property could be perceptible—which is of course not to say there can be no other way to know its presence.

we can take moral properties to be anchored in the natural world and perceptible by their naturalistic grounds.

———————

The theory I have advanced here suffices to explain how ethical objectivity is possible. It provides for the possibility of our finding intersubjectively accessible grounds for at least a wide range of moral judgments—a matter to be explored in more detail in the next two chapters. It also explains how moral knowledge is possible even conceived in a reliabilist framework. The explanation takes account of the distinction between pattern-dependence, as is exhibited by much perceptual knowledge, and premise-dependence, as applied to inferential knowledge. The possibility of moral knowledge by way of perception also does not depend on whether inference can be in some way "implicit." It can be, though we should not take the common phenomenon of the *brain's* processing information, as with facial recognition, to entail that the *person* is implicitly making inferences. The reliability of perceptual beliefs can be accounted for on either interpretation of perception, but it is best accounted for, and explainable in the psychologically simplest way, without taking perception to be implicitly inferential.

If, however, ethical objectivity is possible and if, in addition, there is a kind of moral perception that has high reliability, why is there so much apparently rational moral disagreement? One might think that if there is the kind of intuitive a priori connection that, on my view, holds between perceptible properties and moral properties consequential on them, there would be less disagreement in moral matters or, where there is such disagreement among rational persons, resolution would be less difficult.

Here I can make just three points, each implicit in what has so far emerged. First, just as quite rational persons differ in aesthetic and even perceptual sensitivity, they differ in moral sensitivity and may disagree as a result, even where they witness the same morally right or wrong actions. Second, much moral disagreement centers on propositions that the disputants believe inferentially, and the parties may differ in their standards for sound inference, as indeed scientists may in theirs, or one or another party may draw an invalid inference. Third, even apart from these points, rarely do parties to a moral disagreement respond to identical evidences, for instance exactly the same non-moral facts about well-being or, where disagreement concerns a deed witnessed by both, the same perceptions. Moral disagreement among rational persons, even where each is in some way responding perceptually to the same phenomena, does not show that there is no moral perception or that moral perception cannot often be a basis of knowledge. If it can be a basis of moral knowledge, then at least some moral judgments may be both objectively grounded and, as may be increasingly important in our globalized world, a basis for cross-cultural agreement. How moral disagreement is to be understood on the theory I am developing and how it is connected with intuition and emotion will be among the topics of Chapter 4.

# PART TWO

# Ethical Intuition, Emotional Sensibility, and Moral Judgment

# CHAPTER 4

# Perceptual Grounds, Ethical Disagreement, and Moral Intuitions

THE PREVIOUS CHAPTERS OUTLINE a theory of perception and explain how that theory enables us to explicate moral perception. I have resisted the temptation to subsume moral perception entirely under the ordinary perception of observable natural properties, but I have brought out important respects in which it is similar to that. Moral perception has, for instance, a causal element. It also exhibits some of the phenomenal elements and the discriminative dependence on its object that go with its causal structure. These characteristics are manifested in different ways in different people and may also be colored by elements of culture and upbringing. One person's moral perception may be another's mere behavioral observation. Our normative standards may also influence what we perceive and certainly what we perceptually believe. The bereaved mother and the terrorist will see very different things in a car bombing; the priest and the pimp will see very different things in the offer of money to a desperately poor woman. They may, to be sure, have the same basic perceptions, say of color and shape, voice and movement. But the mother and the priest have moral perceptions that the terrorist and the pimp lack. This makes a great difference in what, overall, they *see*.

If, however, moral perception rests on non-moral perception in the way I have indicated, why is there apparently more disparity in judgment in the moral realm than for ordinary non-moral perception? Chapter 3 briefly described how rational disagreement is possible in ethics, but it left much to be determined in explaining how such disagreement is possible even where moral perception is brought to bear in settling it. I pointed out that not all moral knowledge is perceptual and that not all moral perception produces moral knowledge—it may not even produce moral belief. We should also bear in mind that even in the natural sciences there is much disagreement and that studies of testimonial evidence in criminal matters show that there is considerable disparity in perceptual judgment even among observers of the same scene. But there remains much to say about how rational disagreement is possible in ethics. In addressing this matter, I will consider not only disagreements regarding perceptible moral properties, but disagreements involving moral intuitions and other kinds of moral cognitions. This inquiry is particularly appropriate given that one of my overall aims in this book is to explain how objectivity in ethics is possible and how an intuitionist moral theory can account for rational disagreement without undermining a commitment to the possibility of genuine moral knowledge.

## I. Does Moral Disagreement Undermine Justification in Ethics?

There are many disagreements on moral questions, and in some cases all of the disputants are rational regarding the subject under discussion. Does this show that we are rarely if ever justified in holding a moral judgment, at least when we realize that some comparably informed rational person rejects that judgment?

In understanding disagreements of any kind, it is essential to ascertain whether the disputants differ regarding the same proposition. Sometimes a person rejects what another says without seeing just what that is, perhaps because the language used seems threatening, as where one can tell that one is being accused of something but does not see exactly what it is. We could call this kind of disagreement *illocutionary*, since the disagreement is focused on the other's speech act (the "illocution") and not its content.[1] Illocutionary disagreement may seem to be only a pragmatic phenomenon rather than a substantive difference on the truth-value of some proposition. But this is not all we need to see here. We should distinguish several kinds of disagreement that are important in ethics as elsewhere.

## *Three Kinds of Disagreement*

Suppose a colleague says something indefinite, for instance that my students are unhappy with their assignments. I may reject this description not because I disbelieve the vague claim, which I may simply not accept, without believing it to be false, but because I can think of several propositions that might explain what the speaker has in mind, and I disbelieve each of *those*. One interpretation might be that the assignments are too hard, another that they are too frequent, still another that they are uninteresting. Call this *indefinite disagreement* (the first kind of disagree-

---

[1] For the notion of an illocutionary act, see J. L. Austin's influential *How To Do Things with Words* (Oxford: Oxford University Press, 1962) and (among the many discussions since then) William P. Alston, *Illocutionary Acts and Sentence Meaning* (Ithaca, NY: Cornell University Press, 2000).

ment that concerns me). It is indefinite because the speaker is not clearly committed to any of the specific propositions I disbelieve, nor need I take the speaker to be asserting one of those. We disagree on the vague claim, and there is something more specific on which we differ or would differ if we considered it; but I do not ascribe to my colleague belief of any specific claims. Our disagreement is thus substantive (and not merely verbal), though it is not specific. I reject the assertive speech act—which is why the disagreement may be called illocutionary—but not some particular proposition asserted. It is as if I said, if only to myself: I don't know exactly what you have in mind regarding my students, but the things that come to mind are all propositions I reject.

This example brings us to our main concern here: *content-specific disagreement*, which is the most common kind. This takes two main forms and contrasts with the illocutionary kind, which is indefinite and is a matter of rejecting what is said rather than of believing any specific proposition. Content-specific disagreement is focal, and it occurs when one person affirms something and the other rejects it or at least suspends judgment on it. This need not, however, be *propositional disagreement*, which is probably the most important kind of content-specific disagreement. This kind occurs where the disagreement is over a proposition, which (in cases of such disagreement) I take to be a truth-valued element accessible to more than one mind. But, as is evident from our discussion of the modes of perception and its different kinds of content, content-specific disagreement may be *attributional*—a matter of attributive beliefs and their differing predications—rather than propositional. Let me illustrate this third kind of disagreement.

Suppose we each see a moving shape in the woods ahead and you say, 'It's dangerous—let's not go in there', whereas I say, 'It's not dangerous'. It may be that neither of us has done any more than predicate different properties of the thing we both see but do not recognize, thereby differing in our attributive beliefs. You might believe it to be large and lumbering toward us, while I believe it to be stationary. We might also believe different propositions that are tied to our different points of view and so can be identified only by their believer. You might believe that the shape is like that of a bear *you* saw in a zoo, whereas I may believe that the shape has stubs like those of a tree trunk *I* have seen that was shorn of its branches. These propositions are not expressed by either of us and are not what we disagree on, even if they are part of the source of our disagreement about danger. Still, we may understand each other to ascribe different properties to whatever it is, and that suffices for content-specific disagreement. For a moral example, consider observation of an interview. One of us, struck by diction and body language, may believe the interviewer to be unethical; the other, struck by the animation of the discussion, may believe the interviewer to be simply vigorous and might then be indisposed to make any negative moral judgment on it.

To be sure, even if we disagree regarding an object of discussion only in our ascriptions of properties to it, we are in a *position* to arrive at propositional disagreement as well. We may nonetheless agree that we differ regarding the properties of what we are both willing to describe as the tall shape we see out there. Moreover, it may be that we can rarely *settle* an attributive disagreement without formulating propositions and seeking agreement on them; but here I am explaining what constitutes disagreement. How disagreement arises and how it is settled are different though closely related matters.[2]

Now consider the moral case of the priest and the amoral case of the pimp. The priest sees a woman who, in desperation, may turn to prostitution as demeaned and treated merely as a means. The pimp, by contrast, may see her amorally, as needing to make the best living she can. The cognitive difference here is due to *perspectival disparity*. Each observer has a different perspective from which an indefinite range of propositions will seem true. Each will be disposed to dispute some of the ones accepted by the other, but the perspectival disparity is largely a matter of the categories (in some sense) in which they see the woman. It will tend to produce definite contentual disagreement of both kinds.

The pimp may, to be sure, have certain moral concepts and a good sense of the base properties for them, but may also be *amoral* in one sense: he may have no moral commitments regarding the woman or anyone else and no motivation to act on any moral propositions he may happen to believe. Even if he is not amoral in this sense, he may lack the morally important notions of violation of a person and of treating a person merely as a means. Moreover, supposing he does have these notions, he

[2] There are still other cases of disagreement, and indeed disagreement as considered here (and in the epistemological literature) is a special case of *cognitive disparity*. This notion and related ones are discussed in detail in my "Cognitive Disparities: Dimensions of Intellectual Diversity and the Resolution of Disagreements," forthcoming from Oxford University Press in a collection edited by David Christensen and Jennifer Lackey. An example is difference in degree of conviction. If one person barely believes *p* (or simply accepts it, as with a well-confirmed but disputed scientific hypothesis, without actually believing it) and another says, with great conviction 'Surely *p*', this may occasion illocutionary disagreement and may lead to content-specific disagreement as the two, in discussing the matter, develop different higher-order beliefs, say through differing ascriptions of probabilities.

may not apply them by all the same criteria as the priest, or may simply be insensitive to the evidences that indicate their application. This is in part a matter of moral education. Similarly, just as some people may not have the concept of electricity or, more commonly, do not know, or are not sensitive to, all the main evidences of its presence, the same may hold for wrongdoing.

### Epistemic Peers as Idealized Disputants

One might accept all this and still note that rational persons can disagree in moral matters even when they do have essentially the same relevant concepts and are focusing on the same proposition. Executives may disagree on what bonus is merited by a good employee; legislators may disagree over whether polygamy should be legal; parents may disagree on what punishment is deserved by a wayward adolescent. These truths are important for understanding ethics, but again we must disambiguate: disagreement over prima facie moral appraisal is very different from disagreement over final (on balance) appraisal. We find disagreement among rational persons over whether, say, assisted suicide is wrong on balance; but few if any rational persons disagree over whether killing people is *prima facie* wrong, i.e. (roughly) wrong-making and on balance wrong unless there is an opposing consideration, such as self-defense, of at least equal moral weight. There is a great deal to say about the nature and resolution of moral disagreement, and I have elsewhere examined it.[3] Here I will simply summarize some ways in which, without skepticism,

---

[3] In, e.g., "The Ethics of Belief and the Morality of Action: Intellectual Responsibility and Rational Disagreement," *Philosophy* 86 (2011): 5–29.

we can explain rational moral disagreement among what are called *epistemic peers*.

Consider a possible case of rational disagreement between two people—epistemic peers—who occupy, on the matter at issue (say an attribution of injustice), positions of *epistemic parity*. Roughly, this is to say that on this matter they are (a) equally rational and equally thoughtful and (b) have considered the same relevant evidence equally conscientiously.[4] By contrast with most descriptions of epistemic parity with respect to a proposition, this one explicitly requires that the relevant parties *consider* the evidence and do so *equally* conscientiously. If we require only sharing the same relevant evidence and having the same epistemic virtues (or being equally rational in the matter, which is a similar condition), nothing follows about how fully these virtues are *expressed*, and it is thus possible that, for instance, despite equal epistemic ability and equal possession of evidence, the parties have devoted very different amounts of time or effort or both to appraising the proposition.[5] In that case—exhibiting a kind of *epistemic*

[4] Roger Crisp, in "Intuitionism and Disagreement," in Timmons, Greco, and Mele, *Rationality and the Good*, 31–39, forcefully raises this kind of problem, and I have responded in the same volume, 204–8. I have discussed disagreement further in "The Ethics of Belief and the Morality of Action." Crisp has also developed his position; see "Reasonable Disagreement: Sidgwick's Principle and Audi's Intuitionism," in Hernandez, *The New Intuitionism*, 151–68. Further discussion of Sidgwick's principle is provided by Ralph Wedgwood, "The Moral Evil Demons," in *Disagreement*, ed. Richard Feldman and Ted A. Warfield (Oxford: Oxford University Press 2010), 216–46.

[5] Consider, e.g., a not atypical characterization by Feldman and Warfield, *Disagreement*, meant to capture (as it surely does) a notion common in the literature: "[P]eers literally share all evidence and are equal relative to their abilities and dispositions relevant to interpreting that evidence" (2). Cf. Jennifer Lackey's characterization in "Disagreement and Belief Dependence," in Feldman and Warfield, *Disagreement*, 274. She presupposes in the context (as do many studies of peer disagreement) that consideration of the proposition by

*asymmetry*—disagreement may be readily resolved by an equally conscientious consideration of the relevant evidence. Particularly where we are concerned with the whole range of significant cognitive disparities, it is important that parity be understood to have a non-dispositional element—for our purposes, actually considering relevant evidence in relation to the proposition in question. This element provides a way to account for important disparities that might not be evident in a peer disagreement in which no consideration, or only differentially conscientious consideration, of the relevant evidence occurs.

Let me illustrate. If I believe that a colleague with whom I disagree satisfies (a) and (b), this may prevent me from concluding that I am clearly right. It *should* prevent dogmatism about my own correctness. The possibility that (a) and (b) are jointly realizable in rational moral disagreement should be granted, but it should be stressed that—as skeptics might be the first to emphasize—it is very hard to be justified in believing that someone else satisfies (a) or (b) or, especially, both. The breadth, complexity, and quantity of evidence needed about the other person are great, and error in assessing that evidence is difficult to avoid.[6] It may also be difficult to determine precisely what factors, among the many that may figure in a disagreement, are relevant to it. Evidence is constituted by facts and other elements that are relevant to indefinitely many propositions about which people may

---

both parties *has* occurred and, often, has occurred over time and in a way that requires some thought regarding the relevant evidence.

[6] Two points may help here. First, we may use (a) and (b) to characterize parity *simpliciter*: above all, we widen the scope to include all times and all issues both can consider. Second, though I am discussing only rational persons, the notion of parity would apply to people who are not rational—a complicated case I cannot consider here.

disagree, and the scope of its relevance is not written on its face. In practice, we may be at most rarely justified in believing anyone to be an epistemic peer on a given point at issue. This applies especially to ascriptions of epistemic parity regarding complex moral issues.

## Non-evidential Sources of Disagreement

There is at least one other relevant set of variables. One variable is potentially influential background theories a disputant may hold, such as skeptical ones or ethical theories with myriad implications for the kinds of cases in dispute. Another variable is beliefs that bear on the matter in question or may simply influence a person on it, including "background beliefs" such as prejudicial beliefs that may not surface in the discussion or in the reflections of either party, say that highly educated people are more reliable in moral matters. Beliefs need not even be conscious to influence other cognitions, and the same holds for pro and con attitudes.

Still another variable is difference between disputants in conceptions, especially normative ones, that may affect assessment of an issue without even coming to consciousness. Consider the effects of reading philosophical ethics, say in Aristotle or Confucius in the virtue ethics tradition, Kant or Ross in the deontological tradition, or Bentham and Mill in the utilitarian tradition. We are also influenced by ethically significant novels, such as those of Jane Austen, Charles Dickens, and Fyodor Dostoevsky. Two people can be equally rational and consider the same evidence for a proposition, $p$, but differ in the background cognitions and conceptions they bring to the assessment of that evidence. Such background elements may include religious convictions or theoretical commitments, say to Calvinism, skepticism, or epistemological coherentism. One could include such background factors in "total evidence," but I use 'evidence' more specifically (the influence of background factors on a belief may in any event be only causal rather than justificatory, in which case they are not functioning as evidence for the belief).

Still other factors must be taken into account to achieve a good understanding of rational disagreement. In addition to the difficulty—especially in complex cases—of acquiring justification for believing someone else (a) to have considered the same relevant evidence, (b) to have done so equally conscientiously, (c) to be equally rational in the matter, and (d) to be free of background cognitions that reduce the person's overall justification regarding $p$, there are at least three further factors. One is that someone else's disbelieving $p$ is itself a reason, *for* a person who rationally believes $p$, to doubt that the other is correct in denying $p$ or is a full-scale epistemic peer in the matter.[7] The second is that we are better positioned to make a critical appraisal of our own evidence and of our responses to it than of anyone else's evidence or responses to that evidence.[8] Other things equal, then, we are better justified in our assessment of our own basis for be-

[7] To be sure, unless it is rational for us to *take* ourselves to be rational in believing $p$ (which is not to imply that we must in fact have any such higher-order belief), we may not rationally take ourselves to have a reason to consider the disputant incorrect in denying $p$. But that point is consistent with our simply having such a reason.

[8] The reference to evidence here must be taken to designate mainly grounds of an internal kind, such as the "evidence of the senses." For evidence conceived as publicly accessible supporting fact, I am not suggesting that any one person is necessarily in a better position than another to appraise it, though we may still have a kind of intrinsic advantage in appraising our *response* to it. But for assessing rationality the central concern is the person's experience, memory impressions, reflections, and other internal elements.

lieving $p$ and of our response to that basis than in our assessment of the basis of anyone else's believing it or of anyone else's response to that basis. Even when I justifiedly believe someone else has the same relevant evidence and has considered it equally conscientiously and as freely of biasing background cognitions, I may still not be justified in believing that a contrary belief of the other person's is *based on* the evidence. Possessing evidence is one thing; properly responding to it is another. Justified beliefs must be based on evidence adequately supporting their content; otherwise they are not an adequate response to the evidence but merely "in line" with it. Thus, a contrary belief that is not based on our common evidence is (other things equal) a lesser threat to my belief than one that is.

The third factor is that, as we check and recheck our own grounds for a justified belief that $p$ and our responses to them, we tend to *increase* our justification for believing $p$, at least where we retain that belief (but possibly even if, say from a skeptical disposition, we do not retain it). Insofar as we are self-critical and have justified self-trust, as some of us do, our retention of a belief after such scrutiny tends to be confirmatory. The belief survives a kind of test. Thus, the very exercise of critically seeking to establish the epistemic parity of a disputant may give one a justificatory advantage in the dispute. Perhaps we may conclude that other things equal, making a rational conscientious attempt to establish the epistemic parity of a disputant tends to favor the conscientious inquirer, at least where one retains a disputed belief.

## *Is Rational Disagreement a Crippling Problem for Intuitionism?*

These points about rational disagreement are quite general, but they have a particular relevance for ethical intuitionism and the related theory of moral perception presented in this book. Both posit moral knowledge not based on premises. In doing so, they may appear to free at least many intuitive judgments of the need for evidential grounds. But they do not. Moreover, intuitive moral judgments may have just the kinds of evidential grounds we have seen in the case of moral perception; and even though intuitions are non-inferential, they may—again like moral perceptual beliefs—be defended by inferences when a need for justification arises. Being *held* on a non-inferential basis does not preclude being *defensible* on an inferential basis.

Even if (as I doubt) a justified intuitive moral belief might not be defensible by finding plausible *premises* for it, inferences might be enlisted in its defense by way of clarifying it and rebutting criticism of it. This can apply even to self-evident propositions. As will shortly be explained (and is argued in other work),[9] the claim that at least some basic moral principles are self-evident entails neither that comprehendingly believing them implies having indefeasible justification for them, nor that they cannot be justified inferentially. Given this and the other points in this section, I believe that intuitionists (among others) may retain their convictions in the face of rational disagreement provided certain critical standards are met. These standards seem satisfiable, under some conditions, for at least a good many reflective moral agents.

My account of rational disagreement is meant to show that moral knowledge is possible despite the skeptical concerns arising from the possibility of rational disagreement between epistemic peers. If my case is sound, it supports the possibility of moral knowledge—whether of prima facie moral obligations or

---

[9] In, e.g., "Self-Evidence," *Philosophical Perspectives* 13 (1999): 205–28.

of overall moral obligations.[10] I am not ignoring the common kinds of disagreements in ethics, but these are not between people who are epistemic peers in the relevant matter. That point eliminates some of the difficulties that attempted resolution may face. Neither this point nor any made above imply that the possibility of moral perception makes resolving moral disagreements easy or that, by educating one's perceptual sensibilities in ethics, one can become a moral expert.[11] But even the existence of moral and other disagreements that are difficult to resolve does not support skepticism, nor does an objectivistic realism in ethics imply that there must be moral experts in ethics.

My points about rational disagreement apply not only to empirical moral judgments, say singular judgments appraising a specific person or act, but also to self-evident moral principles, such as the kind expressing general prima facie obligation to avoid killing, cheating, lying, and promise breaking.[12] Many of the moral judgments whose status is in question are based on what I have called moral perception. These include many that are intuitive,

[10] Strictly, an overall obligation (an obligation on balance—"final" obligation) is also prima facie but is not merely so. Prima facie obligations are defeasible, but if not defeated they are final.

[11] For discussion of what might constitute a moral expert, see Sarah McGrath, "Skepticism about Moral Expertise as a Puzzle for Moral Realism," *Journal of Philosophy* 108, no. 3 (2011): 111–37. The kind of realism implicit in this book can account for the difficulties she poses for the view that moral expertise is possible. Note that expertise even in scientific matters is neither required for achieving scientific knowledge nor an attainment guaranteed simply by acquiring a scientific education.

[12] As I have noted in many places, the self-evident may be withholdable, even disbelievable. This is important for explaining how competing theorists, such as moral "particularists," can deny self-evident moral principles of the kind I defend in *The Good in the Right*. How this denial is consistent with rationality is explained in my "Intuition, Inference, and Rational Disagreement in Ethics," *Ethical Theory and Moral Practice* 11 (2008): 475–92.

but intuitive moral judgments also include many that are not perceptual in kind. It is time to consider the intuitive category, its relation to moral perception, and how that relation bears on rational retention of moral intuitions in the face of disagreement.

## II. The Concept of an Intuition

Disagreement occurs at all levels, including that of intuition, though of course one may hope that at least where intuitions are difficult to support by argument—rare though such cases may be—our disagreements in intuitions are either not common or not major for either practical or theoretical matters. How reasonable is such a hope?

This question cannot be answered unless we transcend a common stereotype of intuition which represents it as a "gut response," a kind of automatic cognitive (and often affective) reaction, not mediated by reflection or assisted by inference. If we detach from our idea of intuition the suggestion of mere emotionality or mere personal preference, then this description may hold for some intuitions. Suppose someone said that believing is an action. My intuitive response to this claim has always been immediately negative. This does not make it a gut response, though perhaps it once was. In any case, just as, in a short moment, one can take in myriad details of a painting, one can quickly appreciate a conceptual classification (such as treating beliefs as actions) and place it in a wide context. Thus, even if gut responses typically are among those that come quickly, the rapidity of a response does not imply that it is a gut response—and certainly not a response that is unjustified or does not arise from a background of considerable understanding.

Rapidity of response is not characteristic of all intuitions, for some of the same reasons that indicate why it is not characteristic of all perceptions. Some intuitions emerge only upon reflection, and even some that do arise immediately on considering something are quickly replaced by other intuitions as consideration continues or passes into critical reflection. Imagine that you have to decide whether to cease life support for your terminally ill father, who has never addressed the matter. You will likely reflect on his values, his reactions to relevantly similar cases among relatives, and so on. You may need quite some time, even more than one sitting. When you feel you have a sufficiently informed picture of his values and of what is best for him—a picture sometimes obtained only by imagining a kind of narrative of his life—it may seem to you that you should not allow further life support. If this impression is an intuition, it is non-inferential; but as the example shows, that does not entail its being a gut response.

A cognition can be non-inferential, then, even when its basis contains rich information, perhaps including propositions that can be harnessed as premises to support it. Being non-inferential, moreover, does not entail that an intuition arises independently of inferences in the background, as where one infers facts about medical consequences from what one reads about the available treatments and only then intuitively sees what should be done. We may need ladders to ascend to a plateau, but from there we may be able to reach the summit by a direct path. The path may be long and laborious but may show us a wide view. Understanding a problem, comprehendingly reading a passage, and appreciatively viewing a painting may be similar. Intuition, like understanding, may also come slowly and only when we have taken a long and wide view.[13]

### Five Notions Important for Understanding Intuition

An account of intuition should clarify at least five related notions. Let me characterize each briefly and in that light indicate how some of the notions figure in ethical intuitionism as I conceive it.

*Cognitive intuition.* This is the most common kind of intuition considered in ethical literature: it is intuition *that p* (a proposition), say that a friend deserves an apology for an offensive remark or, to take an ethical generalization as an example, that one should not accept a major gift from a former student whom one must again teach in the future. In the latter case, at least, the intuitive proposition could be subsumed under a moral rule, say one to the effect that we should not do things that produce risky conflicts of interest. But subsumability under a rule need not prevent a proposition from being the object of an intuition, any

---

[13] After writing this I read a recent paper by Patricia Greenspan which makes the related point that "[E]motions can serve as rational barriers to *discounting* reasons." See "Emotions and Moral Reasons," in *Morality and the Emotions*, ed. Carla Bagnoli (Oxford: Oxford University Press, 2011), 40. This holds for intuitions too; e.g., an intuition about a sick father might lead one both to recognize and to give adequate weight to reasons implicit in his values, some of which one might have difficulty articulating at the time one's moral intuition takes shape. My account of the evidential value of emotion in Chapter 6 will show how, in the same non-inferential way, emotions can respond similarly to reasons, often in concert with intuition. But whether or not one articulates reasons, intuition may reflect discernment of their weight, much as we may take account of multiple elements in a poem or a painting as we intuitively interpret and judge it.

more than there need be one route, or only indirect routes, to a given destination. Moreover, some who would have the intuition might not accept any such rule—at least antecedently to reflecting on such concrete instances and generalizing from them.[14]

*Objectual intuition.* This is, roughly, direct apprehension of either (a) a concept, such as that of obligation, or (b) a property or relation, such as the property of being a promise, the property of being unjust, or the relation of entailment. As a kind of objectual knowledge, such intuitions are in a sense *epistemic.* They may also be considered cognitive, though not propositional, but I prefer to reserve the term 'cognitive intuition' for intuitions with propositional objects. In a sense to be explored below, objectual intuition may be conceived as a kind of intellectual perception.

*Intuitiveness.* This is a property primarily of propositions, but it is also predicated of claims, concepts, arguments, and other intellectual phenomena. Applied to a proposition, it is equivalent to the proposition's being *intuitive*—having the property of evoking (under certain conditions) what might be called *the sense of non-inferential credibility* (this notion may be relativized, for instance to persons of a certain description or to a certain level of understanding needed for the intuitive sense to be manifested). That sense is roughly equivalent to the sense of a proposition's (non-inferentially) seeming true—seeming true on the basis of its content, whether alone or viewed in the context in which the proposition is entertained or considered, where this impression of truth does not derive from any sense of the proposition's being

---

[14] Cf. Ross's remarks on intuitive induction in chap. 2 of *The Right and the Good.* Despite the term 'induction' he seems to allow for non-inferential formation of the relevant general belief arising from apprehending instances of one or more crucial properties figuring in the proposition believed.

supported by a premise. This sense of its seeming true normally produces an inclination to believe it.[15] (The normality qualification presupposes reference to a rational person who has at least a minimally adequate understanding of the proposition in question.)

*Propositional intuition.* This is intuition conceived as a proposition taken (by the person using the term) to be *intuitively known* or at least intuitively justifiably believed, say that what is colored is extended or (for some) that capital punishment is wrong. We can imagine someone saying to colleagues on a committee writing an ethics code for a corporation, 'Let's jot down the various intuitions about harassment that have been expressed and see if we can frame a definition for our code of ethics'. Here, intuitions are constituted by propositions, though in these contexts the term may be loosely used non-factively, implying only a presumption of truth. Hence, unlike cognitive intuitions, propositional intuitions are abstract, non-psychological elements and (on most but not all uses) include only truths.[16]

*Apprehensional capacity.* This is intuition as a rational capacity—*facultative intuition*, for short—a kind that is needed for philo-

---

[15] One might think intuitions are constituted by "a subclass of inclinations to believe," as argued by Joshua Erlenbaugh and Bernard Molyneux, "Intuitions as Inclinations to Believe," *Philosophical Studies* 145 (2009): 89–109. It seems to me that an entailment here is the most that can be claimed, at least on the plausible assumption that we are speaking of (occurrent) phenomenal states and may take inclinations to believe as dispositional in nature.

[16] Moore said of propositions about the good, for instance, that "when I call such propositions 'Intuitions' I mean merely to assert that they are incapable of proof." See *Principia Ethica*, x). See also Wilfrid Sellars, *Science and Metaphysics* (London: Routledge & Kegan Paul, 1968), for his use of 'intuiteds' to designate intuited propositions (this category is wider than Moore's in that he intended to use 'intuition' as he here characterizes it for propositions that are not only true but also self-evident).

sophical reflection and manifested in relation to each of the other four cases. It is roughly a non-inferential capacity by whose exercise what is intuitively believed or known is believed or known. Ethical intuition, like logical intuition, is a special dimension of this capacity.

Intuitions with propositional objects (cognitive intuitions) will be my main concern. But the other notions will also be considered, and we gain clarity by distinguishing them from the former and connecting them with those in ways I shall shortly illustrate.[17]

### *The Analogy between Intuition and Perception*

There is much to be learned from conceiving facultative intuition as analogous to the "faculty" of perception and, correspondingly, intuitions as analogous to perceptions. Take seeing as a paradigm of perception. Intuitive apprehension is analogous to seeing. First, it has objects, typically, or at least most importantly for our purposes, concepts and properties. (We need not here discuss what kinds of objects these are, but I assume they are both abstract and in some way connected with linguistic usage, and they are surely accessible through understanding that usage.) Second, in addition to simple apprehension—apprehension *of*—there is also apprehension *to be* (attributive apprehension), and apprehension *as: aspectual apprehension*. The former, apprehension simpliciter, is *de re* (roughly, of the thing that is its object) and apparently does not entail belief, as where a small child apprehends, in an elementary way, the wrongness of smashing a toy but does

---

[17] Most of these notions are discussed in *The Good in the Right*, e.g. 32–39, 48, and 208, note 37. But it contains little explicit treatment of intuitive seemings.

not have a propositional belief that this is wrong or (conceptually) see it *as* wrong. The child may have a sense, perhaps arising from seeing siblings scolded for similar things, that the act is to be avoided, a sense that is potentially motivating; but the child may still lack a concept of wrongness. Attributive and aspectual apprehension entail at least some degree of understanding of the property the object is apprehended to have, or as having, say the wrongness of smashing the toy, but I take conceptualization to be something more than the minimal degree of such understanding, which may be mainly a matter of discriminative responsiveness.

The third point here concerns the connection between an apprehension and an intuitive seeming. Given an apprehension of a type of act, as where we are considering what to do and we envisage various possible acts, it may also intuitively seem to us *that* (for instance) a kind of act in question is wrong. This is a propositional seeming. Fourth, we may, on the basis of this seeming, believe that such acts are wrong. Fifth, if this belief is true, then we intuitively see (apprehend) that the act is wrong. Such true doxastic intuition, a case of intuitive belief, would at least normally constitute intuitive knowledge. The same points hold for an apprehension of a concrete action, though apprehension implies not mere observation of the action but having at least a sense of certain of its properties, say its being a promise breaking or a truth telling in the face of temptation to lie.

We thus have, with intellectual perception as with sensory perception, simple, attributive, aspectual, and propositional perception: (1) apprehensions *of* the relevant object or kind of object, such as the act-type, lying; (2) apprehending the object to have a property, say seeing intimidating interviews to be unfair; (3) apprehensions of the object *as* something, for instance of a kind of act as wrong; and (4) apprehensions *that* the object is something, say, that intimidation is unfair. Simple and attributive apprehensions have the same kind of veridicality as perceptions of concrete objects: I assume that there really are objects of intellectual apprehension which may have properties we apparently apprehend in considering them. Aspectual apprehensions may or may not embody beliefs; but, as also holds with propositional apprehensions, when they do, they commonly represent knowledge.

Are there, as the perceptual analogy suggests, apprehensional counterparts of illusion and hallucination? Might someone mistakenly (illusorily) apprehend the property of redness as coming in precisely discrete shades in concert with its discrete wavelengths? This would be a misapprehension but could still be *of* red, somewhat as visually misperceiving a glass's round rim as elliptical is, though an illusion, still seeing that rim. An analogue of hallucination is more difficult to delineate. Mere possibilia, such as mythological beasts like chimeras, are apprehensible; thus, if we assume that hallucinatory perceptions have no object at all, then to understand them we must focus on something like thinking of a round square.[18] But how could one apprehend "round-squarely," even granting that no false belief is implied? Perhaps someone could apprehend each element with a false sense of their unity. One could perhaps speak of a hypothetical object here, analogous to an object that might be posited for hallucinations, but this is not the place to develop the idea. It is enough that the analogy between intuition and perception is extensive. Let us now explore its application to justification.

---

[18] For detailed discussion of the ontological and other aspects of hallucination (as well as an account of the a priori that supports intuitionism), see chaps. 1, 2, 5, and 6 of *Epistemology*.

Where something's seeming to have a property is a kind of intellectual impression and not a belief, we may speak of an *intuitive seeming*. An intuitive seeming, like a sensory seeming of the kind that occurs when one views the rim of a glass from an angle, may generate a belief with the same content. But where there is no need to form a belief or to make a judgment, and especially where one's concentration diminishes after the seeming arises, a seeming may remain just that. But commonly, you respond to reflections aimed at arriving at an answer to a question by forming a belief that is intuitive—this is a *doxastic intuition*.[19] The propositional content of a doxastic intuition will typically seem true to its possessor upon being entertained, but no such seeming is a necessary *prior* to forming a doxastic intuition.

An intuitive seeming can evidentially support, and can causally produce or sustain, a doxastic intuition, but not every intuitive seeming does either of these things. A counterexample to one's view may be like this. It may be felt as seeming to indicate a truth, but not evoke conviction, at least not immediately. The more we have invested, the more we tend to resist devaluation.

[19] For Walter Sinnott-Armstrong *moral* intuitions are all doxastic: "I define 'moral intuition' as a strong immediate moral belief." See "Framing Moral Intuitions," in his *Moral Psychology*, vol. 2, *The Cognitive Science of Morality* (Cambridge, MA: MIT Press, 2008), 47–76 (47). Cf. the view of Paul Thagard and Tracy Finn concerning what they consider representative moral intuitions: "The intuitions that killing and eating people is wrong and that aiding needy people is right are *judgments* of which we usually have conscious awareness" (emphasis mine). See "Conscience: What Is Moral Intuition?" in Bagnoli, *Morality and the Emotions*, 151. They conceive intuition as equivalent to (or at least entailing) judgment. I find this conception too narrow, though I agree that one can have an intuition dispositionally, as where it is stored in memory—and one can even have it in focal consciousness without being aware *that* one has it or aware *of* it under that description. An instructive related discussion of intuition, especially as connected with emotion, is Peter Railton's "The Affective Dog and Its Rational Tale," forthcoming in *Ethics*.

Furthermore, not every doxastic intuition arises from or is based on an intuitive seeming, though it would be at best unusual to have an intuitive belief (as opposed to, say, an inferential belief), which is, for the person in question, perceptibly inconsistent with an intuitive seeming.

An intuitive seeming implies a felt inclination to believe; the inclination is characteristically based on a phenomenal sense of something's having a property. It is analogous to a perceptual inclination to believe, as where seeing a property inclines one to believe something to the effect that the object in question has it. Beliefs that are perceptibly inconsistent with the truth of a person's intuitive seeming would tend to create a sense of tension. That tension is a kind that a rational person tends to avoid and, if it should arise, to try to resolve. Resolution often occurs through giving up one or the other intuitive element, but such tensions may also lead to giving up a standing belief. (I will say more about this relationship in discussing moral intuitions.)

As already indicated, on any plausible conception of intuitions, they are non-inferential. This might appear to be obviously so for intuitive seemings, since they may appear to be the wrong kinds of elements to be premise-based. But perhaps sense can be made of one seeming's being based on another in at least a quasi-inferential way, as where a person seems anxious on the basis of seeming to be preoccupied with possible failures in a plan you are jointly making. Should we say, then, that a non-doxastic seeming could be inferential at least where the premise is another seeming? This would be misleading. Where one such seeming is based on another of the same kind, we have a close analogy, not to one belief's being inferentially based on another (a premise-belief), but rather to the relation that non-basic perception bears to basic perception.[20] If someone's seeming to me upset is based on the person's seeming to me fidgety, I need not have an inferential belief or inferential seeming as a result and certainly need not have actually drawn an inference. Rather, the seeming fidgetiness is part of a pattern to which this seeming to be upset is a response.

The most important point about intuitions in relation to inference is that they are *direct responses* to something the person sees or otherwise senses or considers, not intellectual responses to a premise that, for the person in question, is in some sense prior to the intuited proposition. The complexity of the object, pattern, or even narrative, to which intuitions (including seemings) respond does not imply that they are inferential. Complexity in what one perceives or considers does not imply forming (or having) premise-beliefs regarding it.

This ascription of non-inferential directness to intuitions goes well with the paradigmatic status of intuitions whose objects are luminously self-evident axioms, though there are also clear cases of intuitions whose contents are not self-evident. Among those who use the notion of intuition discriminatingly, it is widely agreed that it is by intuition that we see the truth of such self-evident propositions as that if all human beings are mortal, and we are all human beings, then we are all mortal.

[20] This is not to deny that one can draw an inference and arrive at a proposition that seems to one true, but (perhaps from a skeptical disposition) one does not believe. Nor should it be denied that one can both inferentially believe that *p* and find *p intuitive*. Finding a proposition intuitive does not require any particular route either to considering it or to believing it if one does; and inferring a proposition is consistent with either disbelieving it (as where one is deducing a contradiction to refute an opposing view) or, by contrast, with its seeming true to one without one's accepting or believing it.

### The Self-Evident and the Obvious

In part because the paradigms of self-evident propositions are both intuitive and obviously true, it is important to see that neither obviousness nor even intuitiveness is essential to them. Consider the proposition that the mother-in-law of a spouse of a person's youngest sibling is that person's own mother. This takes most people some time to see to be true, but it is evident *in itself*, without the need for a premise. It is thus not obvious (even for the same people who can see its truth and later *come* to find it self-evident and even obvious). That point is confirmed by how intuitive it seems to us once we see *how* it is true. A self-evident proposition, then, can be far from obvious yet seem obvious to us once we see its truth on the basis of an adequate understanding of it. The concept of self-evidence in question—and most appropriate in ethical theory—is this:

> Self-evident propositions are truths such that (a) in virtue of adequately understanding them one has justification for believing them (which does not entail that all who adequately understand them *do* believe them), and (b) believing them on the basis of adequately understanding them entails knowing them.[21]

This account makes clear not only why a self-evident proposition need not be obvious but also why it may be withheld or even disbelieved by at least some people.[22] For even when a self-

---

[21] My "Self-Evidence" contains a more detailed account of this concept of self-evidence than *The Good in the Right*. I should add that we might also speak of *full* understanding to avoid the suggestion that adequacy implies sufficiency only for some specific purpose. Neither term is ideal, but "full" may suggest maximality, which is also inappropriate.

[22] Obviousness is relative in a way self-evidence is not: what is self-evident, as my account makes clear, is justifiably believable by anyone who adequately understands it; but what is properly called obvious is understood to be readily seen to be true *by a kind of person* whose comprehensional level is presupposed in

evident proposition that is not obvious is considered by someone, it may not be *psychologically compelling* for that person, as
are, for most normal adults, such simple analytic truths as that
if *x* and *y* are of the same height and *x* is five feet tall, then *y* is
also five feet tall. A psychologically compelling proposition is one
such that adequately understanding it and simultaneously considering it entails believing it. The obvious self-evident truths are
compelling. Such examples as my in-law case show, however, that
we can fully comprehend a self-evident proposition and still need
time to reflect on its content, say on the relationships it expresses,
before we believe it. Clearly, then, not all self-evident truths are
*initially* intuitive: intuitive on first comprehending consideration.
I doubt that all of them must be capable of being intuitive at all.
But if that is so, it is not inconsistent with anything I maintain. It
would indeed help to explain the possibility of rational persons'
disagreeing even on certain self-evident propositions.

Return now to the case of the intuition, formed after much
thought, that we should discontinue life support for the terminally ill patient. Not only is the object of this intuition not self-
evident (which it could not be given that the self-evident is a
priori);[23] we must also grant that the belief in question represents
the person's conclusion in the matter. But how can a conclusion
be non-inferential? There are at least two kinds of conclusions:

---

the context in which the obviousness is ascribed to a proposition. We may also
speak of self-evidence *for* a person where this means not 'believed by that person to be self-evident' (as in some uses) but 'self-evident and capable of being
justifiedly believed by that person on the basis of adequately understanding
it'. The latter—appropriately—makes *understanding* self-evident propositions,
though not self-evidence, relative to persons.

[23] That the self-evident is a priori should be obvious from my characterization of it as knowable on the basis of (adequately) understanding it. This holds
of axioms as commonly understood, and that point helps to explain why it is
plausible to take the self-evident as the base case of the a priori, underlying, e.g.,
provability. For an explication of this view, see chaps. 5 and 6 of my *Epistemology*.

*conclusions of inference*, which are premise-based, and *conclusions of reflection*, which are properly so called because they conclude or wrap up a matter on which one has reflected but are non-inferential. Conclusions of reflection may come only after much thinking or minute observation, but may be epistemically as direct as a master conductor's concluding verdict, concerning a violinist playing in a mediocre way at an audition, that the violinist should not be engaged. The conductor may have to listen for several minutes, but the intuitive conclusion may be based on an overall response, not on such premises as *that the violinist rushed through the delicate passage in the middle*—there may indeed be no such premises in the judge's mind. A piece played without "mistakes" is not thereby played well. A performance having only parts that are beautifully played, like a painting composed only of beautiful parts, may fail to be beautiful.[24]

### III. Intuitions as Apprehensions

Some of our examples show that moral intuitions can have general propositions as their objects, for instance the proposition that there is a prima facie obligation not to kill people. There are also philosophical intuitions, say that believing is not a process.

---

[24] Note that even a self-evident proposition may be a conclusion of reflection and that understanding it may involve inference. Consider this theorem: If $p$ entails $q$, $q$ entails $r$, and not-$r$, then not-$p$. Someone unfamiliar with formal logic may have to realize, by inferring it from $p$ *entails* $q$ and $q$ *entails* $r$, that $p$ entails $r$, in order to see (via the formal truth corresponding to modus tollens) the truth of the theorem. But that $p$ entails $r$ is entailed by the self-evident theorem; it is not a premise for that theorem but an implication of it, nor do we need a separate premise to see the truth of the theorem. In "Self-Evidence" (cited earlier) I call this an *internal* inference and explain how it differs from the external kind that indicates premise-dependent knowledge and justification.

It is plausible to take such general and philosophical propositions to have as constituents (even if not their only constituents) the concepts they are in some sense about, at least in the sense that they reflect facts concerning those concepts. One kind of intuition is what I have called simple: apprehension of a concept, a property, or a relation, where these are viewed as abstract entities. Consider, for instance, poor logic students. We may say of them that they have trouble apprehending the concept of validity or have too few or misguided intuitions about specific entailments (an analogue of perceptual illusions, wherein there is contact with the object perceived but a false impression about it); and we may say, of good students in ethics, that they readily apprehend fittingness relations. Here the analogy is to simple perception but, with intuition, the objects—entailment and fittingness relations—are abstract.

If the analogy between intuitive apprehension and moral perception is as far-reaching as I suppose, then just as one can see the injustice of a deed or the goodness in a person, one may apprehend the concept of injustice or that of personal goodness. Indeed, might the perceptions of the corresponding properties be a normal route—perhaps the only ordinary route—to apprehension of the corresponding concepts?

Here is how that might be so. Apparently, from a conceptual and epistemological point of view, there is a progression—one that seems to correspond to normal human development—in which the first stage is sensory acquaintance (normally of a perceptual kind) with properties and an ability to discriminate some from others; the second is conceptualization of the properties in question, a stage that makes it possible to apprehend them in a conceptual way, which entails an appropriate grasp of their generality; and the third (which presupposes but need not come later than the second) is framing propositions in which the concepts figure—*exercising* the concepts, we might say—as where one has the thought that slapping other people is wrong.[25] The process may be arrested at any stage, but it is commonly completed.

Where moral perceptions and, especially, moral intuitions are in question, it may seem that my account is too heavily cognitive and that motivation should be given a larger role in understanding moral intuition. Normal moral agents are, after all, motivated to avoid what they intuitively believe to be injustice and are motivated to seek, maintain, support, honor (or the like) what they intuitively believe to be good. I see no need to build motivation into the account of either moral perception or moral intuition, but I have made ample room for a strong if contingent connection between moral intuition and motivation to act accordingly. There may be a non-contingent connection between these *in* rational persons, or at least rational persons in whom there is a high degree of integration between cognition and motivation.[26] Some moral intuitions and many moral perceptions—which have the phenomenal vividness that goes with perception and that need not belong to intuition—are no doubt motivating. This may have theological or evolutionary significance. By the grace of God or evolution, or both,[27] we may be sensitive to at least some kinds of

[25] The second stage is comprehensional; the third is active in a way the second makes possible, but it may occur only later when, e.g., there is an occasion to apply the concept.

[26] In "Moral Judgment and Reasons for Action," in my *Moral Knowledge and Ethical Character* (Oxford: Oxford University Press, 1997), I have defended this point in detail and noted much relevant literature.

[27] That biological evolution is compatible with theism is perhaps obvious, and an explanation of its compatibility with various kinds of theism is provided

(intrinsically) good and (intrinsically) bad things, and naturally attracted to the former and averse to the latter. In many people, the moral experience of seeing an injustice tends to be unpleasant, and that of seeing the goodness of a beneficent nursing of a wound tends to be pleasant. But these aspects of our psychological and epistemic constitution are both largely an empirical matter and another topic.

If moral intuitions differ from moral perceptions in their phenomenal character and vividness, they may in many cases be analogous to perceptual beliefs in their "naturalness." This holds especially where intuitions respond to paradigms of the kind important in moral education. Indeed, it may be that just as one cannot help forming certain beliefs upon having certain perceptions, say believing that a growling dog is running toward one if one hears and sees it doing this, so one cannot help having the intuition that someone is doing a wrong if one sees the person drop wet banana peels at the top of a stone staircase in a public square.

If, moreover, we reflect on some of the major stages in moral education, we encounter something that bears on the contrast between nominalistic empiricism and Platonistic rationalism: the ability to generalize, often acquired from observing a single paradigm. Consider a child who takes a model airplane from a friend without permission and is seen by its parents playing with

---

in chap. 10 of my *Rationality and Religious Commitment* (Oxford: Clarendon Press, 2011). For a brief treatment of how morality has apparently evolved in the history of our species, see Frans de Waal, *Primates and Philosophers: How Morality Evolved* (Princeton, NJ: Princeton University Press, 2006). His discussion of loyalty (163–66), which he calls "a moral duty" (165), is representative. Also informative on this topic is Patricia Smith Churchland, *Braintrust: What Neuroscience Tells Us about Morality* (Princeton, NJ: Princeton University Press, 2011).

it. Scolded with a stern utterance of 'This is *stealing!* How would you like it if he took one of your cars?' and ordered to return it to the friend, the child may, with little or no explanation of what stealing is, realize that one must not just take things from people and that returning the plane is required. The child may even see, or be disposed to realize upon thinking about the matter, that one cannot return the plane and take a model truck in its place, or return it and then, by way of replacement, take a toy from a different friend.

The generality of what is learned from experiencing a paradigmatic instance of a concept is commonly almost unlimited. The same child might, perhaps years later, recognize, as stealing, one student's copying a line of poetry composed by another and handing it in as the student's own. This would illustrate cross-categorial generalization from the material to the intellectual. Whatever the explanation of our capacity for generalization, it is a capacity that partly underlies the importance of both perception and intuition in recognizing instances of moral properties.

————

If there is, as I have contended, both perceptual and intuitive knowledge in moral matters, and if the two kinds of knowledge are related as I have maintained they are, then not all our singular moral knowledge, or even all moral cognition regarding specific acts or particular persons, is an application of principles. Indeed, not all moral knowledge even depends on believing principles. Given that so many moral properties are commonly instantiated in virtue of perceptible base properties, and given our intuitive responsiveness to these base properties and to moral properties themselves, moral knowledge need not wait for inference from premises. It is often prior to inference. This priority does not entail that the kinds of beliefs in question are justified or that, when they are, they are indefeasibly so. Their justification may be defeated by a peer disagreement and certainly reduced by that. But neither of these outcomes is entailed by peer disagreement or where, as is far more common, we simply discover disagreement with someone whose judgment on the matter we respect.

This chapter and the previous one have shown that much moral knowledge rests on perception, on intuition regarding ethical questions about actual or envisaged action, or on intuitions concerning hypothetical cases that help us decide what is just or unjust, right or wrong, permissible or obligatory. I doubt that the categorical imperative or the principle of utility would seem plausible apart from confirmation by intuitive results of their application in concrete cases. In any case, everyday moral knowledge is commonly not derived from application of such master principles. In this respect, it seems to be like aesthetic knowledge. The comparison between moral and aesthetic knowledge and other aspects of the similarity between moral and aesthetic cognition is a main concern of the next chapter. It should be clear at this point, however, that in some important if elementary cases, moral knowledge is perceptual. It may certainly arise from perceptually grounded knowledge by a bridge from the descriptive to the normative—especially from a discernment of the descriptive properties that ground moral properties to the moral cognitions that the descriptive properties evidence. That bridge from the descriptive to the moral, and often from *is* to *ought*,[28] has both the strength and the accessibility of the a priori, and, under different conditions, it can sustain both perceptual and intuitive moral knowledge.

[28] Does the point violate "Hume's law," according to which one cannot deduce an *ought* from an *is*? I am not claiming that there are formally valid inferences of the kind in question, nor even that there are informally ("synthetically") valid ones from descriptive propositions to ascriptions of *overall* (final) obligation. The a priori connection is between descriptive propositions and ascriptions of prima facie obligation. But prima facie obligation is important; it is certainly a moral status, and it should lead us to act in accord with it if there is no overriding set of factors. The epistemological point in question is defended in, e.g., chaps. 1 and 2 of *The Good in the Right*.

CHAPTER 5

*Moral Perception, Aesthetic Perception,*
*and Intuitive Judgment*

THE THEORY OF VALUE properly includes aesthetics as well as
ethics, but too few contemporary philosophers have adequately
explored the bearing of aesthetics on ethics. The connections between the two are especially important for understanding moral
perception and moral intuition. There is aesthetic perception, as
opposed to mere perception of an aesthetic object, just as there
is moral perception, as opposed to mere perception of a moral
phenomenon; there is aesthetic intuition, just as there is moral
intuition; and, in aesthetics as in ethics, we find aesthetic disagreements that, even more than moral disagreements, challenge
the view that normative domains have objective standards. Much
can be learned about both ethical and aesthetic judgment from
the comparison between the two realms.

## I. THE ROLE OF INTUITION IN
## AESTHETIC EXPERIENCE

Many aesthetic experiences are perceptual: hearing a sonata, seeing a painting, feeling a sculpture. But not all aesthetic experi-

ences are perceptual. Reading a poem is different. Aesthetic experiences in reading poetry may depend on visual perception,
but are not themselves perceptual, much less visual—unless it is
because the poem evokes visual or other sensory images of aesthetic significance for the reader. The experience may indeed be
much like the experience of rewardingly "hearing" the poem in
silent soliloquy. In a way, the words are heard but not voiced.

To be sure, we might speak of inner perception of the mentally
uttered poetic lines or the picture they may paint of person or a
landscape; but this is not perception in the ordinary sense. It is,
however, *experiential*, and the aesthetic experience is a *response*
to what is experienced. We can best understand the role of intuition in aesthetic experience if we focus on the broad notion of an
aesthetic response rather than on aesthetic perception, which—
even if it is a central case of aesthetic experience—represents a
narrower category.

In many aesthetic responses, intuition figures importantly.
Some aesthetic responses are temporally immediate; but many,
like that of an orchestra conductor listening to a highly competent but uninspiring violinist, take time. As suggested earlier, it
is essential to see that temporal immediacy is not required for
intuition. This holds even for self-evident propositions that are
not obvious but, once they are seen to be true, are highly intuitive
to the person in question. We needn't "just see" what is, at some
point in our thinking about it, highly intuitive for us. Gradual
discernment and even reflection may be required to see an intuitive truth. In cases like this there may or may not be, at the end
of one's consideration of the proposition, a kind of naturalness
in the cognition. Conductors at an audition may mistrust their
intuitions and, for that reason, allow the candidate to play longer

than normal, or they may consult a colleague before making a judgment. Intuitions differ not only in the reflection needed for their formation, but also in other dimensions, including, where they are propositional, the confidence levels they embody toward their propositional objects.

Even where intuitions arise naturally from aesthetic experience and exhibit high confidence, the irresistibility of belief formation common with certain perceptions is very often absent. The counterpart point holds for moral intuitions formed from moral experience. But aesthetic intuitions seem, on the whole, to require more experience and education than do moral intuitions. My contrast between the way perceptual experience, whether moral or aesthetic, gives rise to intuitions and the way it yields perceptual beliefs is not meant to imply that perception *must* produce belief (which I think false). The point is that, given the perceptual presence of certain non-aesthetic, non-moral properties of an object—most notably observable properties—if something or someone raises the question whether it has one of these properties, the perceiver cannot in general resist forming the belief that it does. Seeing a round cloud in the sky above may evoke no belief about it when, though it is in my visual field, I am concentrating on an intellectual problem; but if I am at that moment asked whether there is a round cloud above, it is difficult to resist forming the belief that there is. Here to see almost certainly *is* to believe.

This point about irresistibility of belief-formation in certain perceptual cases is partly a matter of empirical phenomenology and may apply both to some cases of moral perception and to some cases of aesthetic perception. Suppose Evelyn is both morally and aesthetically sensitive. Hearing one person speak offensively to another might, for her, make a perception of wrong-doing irresistible; seeing a dancer wobble during a waltz might inevitably evoke an aesthetic perception of clumsiness. These perceptions are non-propositional, but they might evoke, virtually irresistibly, intuitions that the first person is wronging the second and that the dancer is waltzing clumsily.

One possibility in the moral case is that the intuition is quite confident. It might also yield, perhaps after some reflection, a moral judgment with the same propositional content. That judgment in turn might express moral knowledge. Another possibility is that the perception quickly yields a moral judgment, without first producing an intuition that leads to making the judgment. Whether, if so, the judgment is silent or expressed in a disapproving utterance is a quite different matter—heavily dependent on such pragmatic variables as the context and the relation between the observer and the offender. Moreover, in a moral case like this, or in its aesthetic counterpart, the content of the judgment may be *intuitive* for the person who makes it, even if the judgment does not *arise* from an intuition but from simply seeing something obvious without the phenomenal element that goes with intuition.

## II. Aesthetic and Moral Properties: Comparison and Contrast

The significant analogy between ethical and aesthetic perceptions and intuitions has other aspects we should note. One concerns the relation of aesthetic properties, for instance beauty, delicacy, balance, unity, and enchantment, to their base properties—their grounds. That aesthetic properties are consequential seems virtually as clear as the counterpart point in ethics. Just as an action cannot be brutely wrong but must be wrong in virtue of being, for example, a killing or a lie, a painting cannot be just beautiful or a sonatina just delicate. The painting must be beautiful in virtue of, say, composition and coloring, and the sonatina must be delicate in virtue of a combination of, for instance, melody, harmony, and rhythm. Moreover, it appears that aesthetic properties are like moral ones in being both normative and consequential on descriptive properties.

To be sure, normative terms are not without a *kind* of descriptive power. One can, for instance, *describe* a sonatina as delicate. But this sense of 'describe' is generic. It means something like 'characterize' or even simply 'apply an adjective to'. In that wide sense one can also describe a person as scrupulously just, but this moral property is not what philosophers have considered a descriptive one. There is no easy way to specify what constitutes a descriptive, as opposed to normative, property; but perhaps we can at least say that descriptive properties, when possessed by concrete objects, are causal. This does not seem to me to apply to moral properties, and I doubt that it applies to any normative ones (though its doing so is consistent with virtually every point I make about moral and other normative properties). That an action was obligatory, for instance, is not a proposition about its effects or causes, nor is it an ascription of a causal power to it; and the same applies to attributions of intrinsic (aesthetic) goodness to a poem or a painting.

Another way to see the similarity between moral and aesthetic properties is to note that there is a quite strong supervenience in each case. Specifically, no two actions or persons can be alike in all their non-moral properties and differ in their moral ones, and no two paintings or other artworks can be alike in all their non-aesthetic properties and differ in their aesthetic ones.[1] Consequentiality (described in Chapter 2) is a stronger relation than supervenience in being a *determination relation*. It is instantiated in the aesthetic domain (and others) as well as in the moral. It appears that just as an act's obligatoriness is determined by, say, being promised, a painting's beauty is determined, in some very complicated way, by such non-aesthetic properties as its colors, textures, lines, and shapes.[2]

These metaphysical truths—that both moral and aesthetic properties are supervenient and consequential—seem to me a priori and necessary truths about the moral and aesthetic realms; but the analogies we have noted should not be allowed to obscure some important differences. One is a difference in the kinds of consequentiality relations that occur in the aesthetic and ethical domains. In the aesthetic case, as opposed to the ethical case, the relation of consequential properties to their base properties is not, at least in general, a priori and is probably not in all cases necessary. We may be able to explain, by pointing to its qualities, such as fineness of description and development of a single theme, why a poem by Shakespeare is delicate or unified; but we will not in general be able to frame a priori generalizations to the effect that poems with those qualities (described in general

---

[1] Granted, historical properties are relevant to the value of aesthetic objects. But the value of an aesthetic object need not be, and certainly need not be exhausted by, aesthetic value. The beauty of a sculpture is not a matter of who shaped, textured, and colored it but of the shape, texture, and color it has. A perfect replica would be equivalent in beauty, grace, elegance, and so forth for other aesthetic properties.

[2] For a detailed account of the determination relation in question, see Paul Audi, "Grounding: A Theory of the *In Virtue Of* Relation," forthcoming in the *Journal of Philosophy*.

terms) are unified, or even to the effect that those qualities are delicacy-making or unity-making in the way lying is wrong-making. One hypothesis to explain this is that aesthetic properties are, like final as opposed to prima facie obligation, *organic*—applicable only on the basis of some non-additive combination of aesthetically contributory properties.[3]

## III. The Rule-Governed Element in Ethics and Aesthetics

If, in aesthetics, there are no close analogues of a priori moral principles, it does not follow that there can be no aesthetic principles or rules at all. An important question that arises here is whether there are aesthetic rules and, if so, whether such rules must simply be more vague than moral ones. They apparently are more vague, and this may be partly because they play a different role in our lives. The role of artworks and even of natural beauty in human life is crucial for its quality but is not necessary, or not so in the same way, for our survival in social groups. Without people's conforming, by and large, to ethical standards at least within their own group, human life in society would be unlikely to persist. This does not hold for aesthetic properties; and, in many cases, they (as opposed to the natural properties they are consequential on) are also not as readily accessible to

---

[3] For an informative discussion of how aesthetic properties are related to other kinds and of the extent to which attribution of the former may be appropriately subsumptive, see Richard W. Miller, "Three Versions of Objectivity: Aesthetic, Moral, and Scientific," in *Aesthetics and Ethics*, ed. Jerrold Levinson (Cambridge: Cambridge University Press, 1998), 26–58. Peter Railton's "Aesthetic Value, Moral Value, and the Ambitions of Naturalism" (in the same volume, 59–105) also bears on the basis of aesthetic properties. It is fruitfully compared with Sturgeon's "Moral Explanations," cited above.

perception as are some important moral properties in the kinds of observable cases I have described. Aesthetic properties are, however, similar to overall obligation in being consequential in a way that very often implies the need for training in order to perceive their presence. Consider balance, unity, engagingness, and insight. Here is the first part of Shakespeare's Sonnet 116:

> Let me not to the marriage of true minds
> Admit impediments. Love is not love
> Which alters when it alteration finds
> Or bends with the remover to remove.
>
> Oh no! It is an ever fix'ed mark
> That looks on tempests and is never shaken.
> It is the star to every wand'ring bark
> Whose worth's unknown although its height be taken.

This is fine poetry. Compare it with this parody:

> Let me not to the junction of two lands
> Omit a border wall. Neighbors cannot each other like
> When mixing's indiscriminate. Oh no! Firm hands
> Must we have, to keep us free from strife.
>
> Walls are the mark that guides us in the night,
> The line we trust to keep our fields in sight. . . .

We need not draw inferences from rules to see that this versification is bad poetry. We can articulate defects of it, but their relation to its aesthetic deficiency is not as close as that of, say, unequal sentencing of equal partners in crime is to injustice.

A related point about the aesthetic in contrast with the ethical is that in the former case education and experience may be even more important for the development of the relevant intuitive capacity. But does the fact that cognitions come to people only after training entail that their justification for those cognitions is relative to that training in a sense that makes their intuitions provincial and undermines any claim those intuitions may have to cross-cultural validity? I think not, and this can be confirmed even in mathematics, a field that is paradigmatically cross-cultural. Mathematical education is required even to have certain intuitions; those intuitions are not thereby rendered provincial or limited in evidential significance. In the literary realm, Shakespeare is fully accessible only to those who can comprehend his rich and subtle English; but the aesthetic value of his poetry and drama is not thereby rendered provincial. It can be appreciated by those to whom English is not native, but simply well learned. Indeed, substantial elements in the value of any great poetry can survive translation.

Much as the aesthetic value of a poem can survive translation, the moral value of certain kinds of acts can survive a behavioral analogue of translation. Consider the (prima facie) obligation to express gratitude when someone does something good for us that is not obligatory and not easy. In one culture a bow might be the normal way to thank someone on an appropriate occasion; in another culture some form of words, such as 'thank you', might be the norm, and bowing might be considered sarcastic. Thus, to translate 'thank you' into the language of the culture in which bowing is the norm for expressing gratitude, and to expect the resulting words to constitute a conventional expression of gratitude, would be ethically erroneous. The ineffectiveness of the resulting words for expressing gratitude would not, however, imply substantive moral disagreement between the cultures.

The concept of the obligation to express gratitude, then, is instantiable in multifarious cultural forms. There can be good and bad ethical translations among these forms. The same holds for at least many other obligations. We need not suppose that the difficulty or impossibility of translations in some cases implies that there are no cross-culturally valid standards—expressing genuine moral values—any more than we need conclude that there is no real poem or, more important here, no aesthetic value in the poem as distinct from the plethora of linguistic presentations that the poem, or indeed its value, may have.[4]

## IV. The Reliability of Intuition

Intuition may be usefully compared with perception. Perception is widely considered to be (as I shall assume it is) a broadly reliable "faculty," in roughly this sense (using seeing as our paradigm): if we see a thing, then if, visually and on the basis of our seeing it, it clearly seems to us to have a property, it usually does.[5] Perception is also highly informative, in the sense that if (for instance) we see an object, there are certain things, often a great many, that we can visually know about it. Commonly, we can discern its coloration, something about its shape and texture, its

[4] Much more could be said about the ontology of artworks, but there is no reason to think we must settle for an ontology that undermines the possibility of aesthetic value that is analogous in the suggested way to moral value. Regarding the example of gratitude, if one thinks it represents etiquette rather than ethics, I would suggest that in any case the most important standards of etiquette may overlap ethical standards and may be sufficiently analogous to them for our purposes here.

[5] Notice, however, that we cannot validate perceptual beliefs without relying on perception itself. This circularity problem has been examined by a number of epistemologists, notably William P. Alston. See his "Epistemic Circularity," *Philosophy and Phenomenological Research* 46 (1986): 263–90.

location in relation to us, and more. Much could be said here, but my main concern is simply to explore whether ethical intuition, though not itself a kind of propositional perception, is grounded in a similar way and may, in a significant number of cases, be comparably reliable.[6]

We may immediately set aside the cases of plainly factive intuition in which one sees *that* some moral proposition holds and thereby has an intuitive moral belief, say that one person is being unfair to another in negatively evaluating the latter's work. For (at least normally) if one sees that something is so, one knows it is, and it is uncontroversial that cognitions constituting knowledge are a reliable kind. Where propositional moral perception and moral intuition coincide in this way, the propositional object in question is true, however difficult it may be to identify the basis of the perception in a detailed informative way. This is a point that even skeptics may grant, though they may hasten to claim that in moral matters we either never in fact *see* that something is so or, at least, never know or justifiedly believe that we do. The cases of special interest here are those in which someone considers an act or person, whether actual or hypothetical, and forms a moral intuition about the person or act. Given the reliability and

---

[6] Critical discussion of my view is provided by Walter Sinnott-Armstrong in "Reflections on Reflection in Robert Audi's Moral Intuitionism," in Timmons, Greco, and Mele, *Rationality and the Good*, 19–30 (with a response from me on 201–4). Other relevant papers are contained in his three-volume collection from MIT Press (2008). See also Michael R. DePaul, "Intuitions in Moral Inquiry," in Copp, *The Oxford Handbook of Ethical Theory*, 595–623. Sinnott-Armstrong raises further problems for intuitionism, though in this case concerning justification more than reliability, in "Framing Moral Intuitions," cited earlier, and "An Empirical Challenge to Intuitionism," in Hernandez, *The New Intuitionism*, 11–28. A valuable defense of evidential appeals to intuition (given criticism like Sinnott-Armstrong's) is provided by Michael Huemer in "Revisionary Intuitionism," *Social Theory and Policy* 25 (2008): 368–92.

informativeness of perception, we have two counterpart questions about intuition: How reliable is moral intuition? And how informative is the basis on which it rests?

### Intuitions as Responsive to Grounds

We cannot determine, in an a priori and general way, just how reliable moral intuitions are, but once we see the extent to which discrimination and even reflection can underlie them, and once we view moral properties as such that, for a great many of them, their presence is readily discerned given perception or apprehension of their base properties, there is no reason to be skeptical about the epistemic status of all intuitions, and there is some reason to consider many of them sound. Intuitions, though not based on premises, do normally arise from supporting grounds, as opposed, say, to mere cultural conditioning, applications of stereotypes, or wishful thinking. The main kinds of grounds on which ethical intuitions rest—in rational persons with a mastery of moral concepts—are a priori indications of moral properties, for instance non-moral properties such as killing, lying, promise breaking, or, on the positive side, rescuing. These are a priori wrong-making, obligation-making, or good-making.[7] As some of our examples have indicated (and a number of others to come will confirm), the presence of these properties entails, in an ap-

---

[7] I am assuming here a moderate generalism about grounds of moral obligations, on which certain kinds of properties, like killings, always imply prima facie wrongness. This is compatible with holism about overall obligation but not with strong particularism of the kind Jonathan Dancy has defended. I have addressed this controversy and defended my view in "Ethical Generality and Moral Judgment," in *Contemporary Debates in Ethical Theory*, ed. James Dreier (Oxford: Blackwell, 2006), 285–304.

parently a priori way and sometimes by a self-evident connection, that the act in question is, say, prima facie obligatory, or that the thing with a good-making element (say, pleasure in an experience) is prima facie good: roughly, good overall if there is no opposing element of at least equal normative weight.

Aesthetic intuitions are not similarly grounded; there are few if any (substantive) a priori connections between non-aesthetic and aesthetic properties, particularly the positive properties like being delicate or beautiful, as opposed to such negative ones as being clumsy or disunified. This is one reason the reliability of moral intuitions should not be considered wholly on a par with that of aesthetic intuitions. For both kinds of intuitions, however, our reliability can be enhanced by education and experience.

In holding this view, I am maintaining an intuitionist position regarding basic common-sense moral principles, such as the prohibitions of killing, beating, and lying. These posit a wrong-making relation between such non-moral act-properties as killing and the property of being wrong. The relation of such non-moral act-properties to the moral property of wrongness self-evidently obtains. The same holds for the relation of such right-making properties as being a promise keeping to being obligatory. Given the points in our discussion of the self-evident, it is not difficult to see how some people can be superior to others in intuitional reliability: roughly, in the proportion they exhibit (in a broadly normal range of circumstances) of true to false intuitions. People differ markedly in the relevant kinds of discernment, understanding, and sensibility. But even apart from our success in arriving at true beliefs in general, at least our ethical intuitions grounded on a perception or apprehension of the base properties of the moral properties that the intuitions ascribe tend to be true.

Recall the cases of the subtly intimidating handshake and the covertly hostile interview. The intuitions in cases like these are commonly also instances of cognition constituting knowledge; and when they are embedded in propositional perception, they are also instances of propositional moral knowledge.

### Intuitions regarding Overall versus Prima Facie Obligation

If an intuition is that an action is obligatory *overall*, or wrong *on balance*, as opposed to prima facie obligatory or prima facie wrong, then its reliability depends on its taking appropriate account of a complex pattern of factors. Moral intuitions frequently are responsive to the appropriate kind of complex: we often have an awareness of a pattern whose presence implies, for instance, the overall obligatoriness of keeping a promise or the overall wrongness of lying. Think of cases in which a close friend is plainly counting on one's veracity and will be harmed if one lies. A ready awareness of this kind of pattern is possible in part because of what we have retained from moral experience, but the most important point here is that the number of factors relevant to determining overall obligation (and perhaps overall goodness) is often quite small.[8]

If overall obligation is commonly a matter of an organic combination of grounding elements—say, a promise to do something for a friend, together with the promised deed's offending a sec-

---

[8] I have proposed a theory of intrinsic value in "Intrinsic Value and Reasons for Action," *Southern Journal of Philosophy* 41, supplement (2003): 30–56. On the prospects for conceiving intrinsic value hedonistically, see Roger Crisp, *Reasons and the Good* (Oxford: Oxford University Press, 2007), and Fred Feldman, "The Good Life: A Defense of Attitudinal Hedonism," *Philosophy and Phenomenological Research* 65 (2002): 604–28.

ond friend, burdening a third, and causing oneself to miss a rare opportunity for self-development—then it is like aesthetic value in the complexity of the combinatory normative weights of relevant elements. But, in addition to the differences already noted between the moral and the aesthetic in the kinds of connections that link descriptive grounds of normative properties to the possession of those properties, there is also a difference in complexity. Whereas it is common for a moral property like obligatoriness or wrongness to have a single main ground such as a promise or the need to render aid to someone injured, it is at best rare that any significant aesthetic property may be reliably ascribed on the basis of a single ground. Granted, a watercolor displaying only a single shade of gray might thereby be visually dull. But this is a rare kind of painting, and visual dullness is a special (and often simple) kind of aesthetic property. Most aesthetic properties—especially the positive ones such as beauty, elegance, and unity—are consequential on a complex of base properties. That complex is often not readily describable, and sometimes the properties are too numerous for the observer to list. Art can be required to describe art.

Aesthetic intuition, then, even when refined and based on extensive experience, is not precisely analogous to moral intuition. But both are responses to discernible patterns, and both can often be justified by appeal to elements in those patterns. The similarities support the idea that intuitive responses are not results of unconscious inferences. The relevant patterns are seen or apprehended in a holistic way, not specified by a list of the constituent properties and relations—a list that we would be hard-pressed to compose even in an extended period of time. This does not entail either that justificatory inferences can never be drawn or that, even when they cannot be, the ethical or aesthetic intuitions in question are merely subjective responses lacking any rational basis.

If Ross was correct in *The Right and the Good*, the essential factors determining prima facie moral obligation include considerations of non-injury, veracity, beneficence, and gratitude. (These and other factors will be considered in some detail in Chapter 7.) To be sure, countenancing these as a priori grounds of prima facie obligation leaves open how readily we can determine, intuitively or otherwise, what our final obligations are. I grant that (as utilitarians would insist) we should be properly concerned with whether, in a world with as much suffering as ours has, we are doing enough for others to fulfill our obligation of beneficence. But the complexity that these variable factors introduce does not prevent our often having adequate grounds for believing that we ought overall to avoid certain harms to others, abstain from lying, and make charitable donations.

If these points are correct, we may also consider the capacity for ethical intuition to be an informative faculty, in this sense: given a consideration of a morally significant act or situation, a person who understands moral concepts and is aware of the base properties for the relevant moral properties exhibited by the act or situation is in a position to have intuitive knowledge of those moral properties or at least to have justification for propositions attributing them to the act or situation. Roughly, in people with an adequate understanding of moral concepts, the discernment of the non-moral properties on which moral properties are consequential tends to be highly informative and is a basis for intuitive knowledge and justification. Given my having the concept of beneficence (or at least given my having beneficent inclinations), if I observe someone slip on an icy sidewalk and bleed from the forehead, I will perceive an obligation to render aid and will tend to judge that I should help. My obligation to help is consequential on the combination of relievable distress and my own ability to relieve it. My obligation may be overridden by a weightier one or even canceled by the preemptive action of someone else who quickly takes over and gives aid; but the obligation is initially both present and quite perceptible. When obligation is overridden by a conflicting weightier one, the overridingness may be something not perceived but intuitively realized, often only after reflection.

Discernment of the base properties of moral properties is not the only ground of moral knowledge and moral justification. For instance, nothing prevents us from bringing a sound moral principle (such as, for many moral philosophers, some version of the categorical imperative or of the principle of utility) to bear on a situation and arriving at moral knowledge by subsuming an act under such a principle. But such subsumptive moral knowledge is not the basic kind, even of singular propositions. This is not to assume without argument that conforming to the categorical imperative, for instance by acting from a maxim that accords with it, or acting on knowledge that one is maximizing utility, are not bases of moral knowledge or of moral justification at all. But moral knowledge by subsumption is inferential knowledge based in part on the relevant generalization; it is not a direct response to the base properties and consequentiality relations that ground the truth of that generalization.

––––––––

The previous chapter brought out important ways in which perceptual and intuitive knowledge in moral matters are related. This chapter shows how singular moral knowledge is like singular aesthetic knowledge in resting on a response to properties which ground the truth of the normative propositions known. In both cases, moreover, responsiveness depends on a kind of discernment in which people vary, both in the scope of their discernment and in the speed and reliability with which it yields perception, intuition, or judgment. This similarity transcends an epistemological difference in the realm of general knowledge: the aesthetic domain is unlike the moral domain in not being governed by comparable a priori principles, if by any a priori principles at all. But this difference does not undermine the crucial point of comparison: in both the moral and the aesthetic cases our knowledge has an experiential basis, and in neither case need it depend upon inference from principles (perhaps in aesthetic cases it cannot so depend). In both realms, moreover, the basis of singular judgments can be intersubjectively sharable and a ground for objective justification.

# CHAPTER 6

# Emotion and Intuition as Sources of Moral Judgment

MORAL PERCEPTION IS POSSIBLE for virtually any normal person with an elementary mastery of moral concepts. It is common among people with highly discriminative moral sensibilities. It characteristically makes many moral propositions intuitive for the perceiver. It is a major route to moral intuition, and it often yields moral knowledge. But moral perception is by no means the only route to moral intuition or moral knowledge. Reflection is another route. Its subject matter may be concrete, as where a practical decision must be made regarding life support for an accident victim; it may be abstract, as where the topic is philosophical, say a question of whether promise breaking is always prima facie wrong; and in either case reflection may be what yields moral intuition about its subject matter. Moral intuitions may also arise in a quite different way: from emotion. How this is so, and what evidential value emotions may have in ethical matters, are central concerns of this chapter.

## I. Emotion and Intuition:
## Interaction and Integration

Intuition and emotion are sometimes associated.[1] Some emotions, such as certain misgivings, and perhaps a sense of foreboding, are at least next door to intuitions. Intuitions, especially those constituting insights into others' consciousness, can be vivid and tied to keenly felt emotions, such as compassion. Correspondingly, intuitive people are commonly viewed as people of feeling. But intuitions need not be connected with emotion, as in the case of purely intellectual intuitions; and emotions, such as rage that arises from someone's carelessly crashing into one's car, need not be connected with intuition. Emotion may also differ from intuition in having no definite object, as seems possible in certain instances of free-floating anxiety. In the realms of contemplation and conduct, however, there is a close connection between emotion and intuition.

[1] Thagard and Finn, e.g., say, "Introspection supports the claim that moral intuitions are a kind of emotional consciousness" ("Conscience: What Is Moral Intuition?" 151), though they carefully avoid implying that either intuition or emotion is *irrational*: "[M]oral intuition, like emotional consciousness in general, is not *just* visceral, because our overall interpretation of a scene is colored by cognitive appraisal as well" (152). Although Mark Wynn does not explicitly identify emotion with feeling in the sense in which he associates the latter with intuition, he sympathetically (perhaps with full agreement) cites Schleiermacher's view that "Intuition without feeling is nothing and has neither the proper origin nor the proper force; feeling without intuition is also nothing . . . they are originally one and unseparated" (quoted in Wynn, *Emotional Experience and Religious Understanding*, 66). Wynn's quotation from Quentin Smith is a more recent indication of the association: "In this rejoicing I am experiencing a captivated intuition of the determinately appearing importance of global fulfillment." See Smith's *The Felt Meaning of the World: A Metaphysics of Feeling* (West Lafayette, IN: Purdue University Press, 1986), 64 in Wynn. For a wide-ranging treatment of emotion in relation to intuition, see Sabine Roeser, *Moral Emotions and Intuitions* (Houndmills, Basingstoke: Palgrave Macmillan, 2010).

*Truth and Falsity in Emotion and Intuition*

Consider moral emotions, for instance indignation, some kinds of disapproval, and certain types of resentment. These are not uncommon in everyday life. Are there intuitions that are equivalent to these or other emotions? One obstacle to any such identification is that emotions are strictly speaking not truth-valued (or at best not happily considered truth-valued), whereas at least doxastic intuitions, a very common kind of intuition, are. To be sure, we might speak of false fears where a person fears that an accident will occur but is mistaken. It seems preferable, however, to call such a fear ill-grounded or to call the *person* (or the cognition in question) mistaken.

Suppose, by contrast, that one person fears another's arrival and is correct in expecting that the other will arrive but wrong in taking that to be something to fear. Is the fear true because of the true expectation it embodies, or false because of the misappraisal that underlies it? Neither answer seems quite right. Note too that 'fear' has a non-emotional use: we might speak, for instance, of fearing that there will be no fresh fruit on the menu, when no emotion is involved. Fear is not the only emotion that can have a propositional object. Just as we can fear that a low-flying plane will hit us, we can be angry that the pilot violated the law. But there is no temptation to speak of true or false anger, except perhaps where these terms mean (respectively) something like 'genuine' and 'merely ostensible'.

Granted, there are intuitions, as there are emotions, with non-propositional objects. These are of course not truth-valued. Take intuitions of dishonesty in an examinee or a salesperson. These might have an emotional aspect, such as distrust, but are

not themselves emotions. Attributive intuitions are typically apprehensional, not emotional (though they may lead to emotion);
and propositional emotions, among other emotions—say, indignation *that* someone did not keep a promise—are not themselves
properly considered true or false, as opposed to well-founded or
ill-conceived. Even if propositional emotions might in special
cases be coherently said to be true or false, the many emotions
lacking propositional objects, such as rage and grief, may not be
coherently so described.[2]

## Motivational and Affective Aspects of Emotion

A second obstacle to identifying emotions with intuitions is that
intuitions, unlike emotions, are not intrinsically motivational.
To be sure, in integrated persons—roughly those whose cognitions, motivation, emotions, and other intentional elements are
mutually coherent—many kinds of intuitions do produce or are
characteristically *accompanied* by motivation to act accordingly.
But an intuition about, say, the validity of a logic-book argument
with trivial content, need not be motivating.

The elements of feeling and motivation in emotion do not prevent their admitting of rationality, and emotions may be well-
grounded or ill-grounded. When Shakespeare's Othello describes

---

[2] This is not to deny that a proposition can expresses a kind of cognitive
norm important for the constitution and rationality of the emotion. Consider
what Robert C. Roberts calls a "defining proposition" for an emotion; e.g., "Relief's defining proposition is this: '*It is important that X be in condition Y, though
X was not, or might not have been, or was not known to me to be, in condition
Y*'." See *Emotions: An Essay in Aid of Moral Psychology* (Cambridge. Cambridge
University Press, 2003), 279. For a recent statement of the tripartite conception, with detailed discussion of emotions in art, see Berys Gaut, *A Philosophy
of Cinematic Art* (Cambridge: Cambridge University Press, 2010), esp. 244–52.

himself as having "loved not wisely but too well" (act 5, scene 2), he is not just providing a poetic figure. Loving wisely is not simply a combination of love with wisdom, and Othello is admitting a defect in his emotion, of a kind connected with its apparently narrow basis and disconnection from the kind of understanding that should guide it. (Early in the play he says, of Desdemona's fascination with his account of his harrowing exploits, "I loved her that she did pity them.") Emotions as well as intuitions are essential for developing an adequate moral epistemology, and they interact. In ways to be described shortly, intuitions are important for understanding emotion, moral judgment, moral perception, and other phenomena of concern in this book.

Although I offer no analysis of the concept of emotion, it should be evident that I conceive emotions (including moral emotions) as multifaceted psychological elements that are normally responses to experience, whether of the outer or inner world, or to the real or merely imagined. Three kinds of constituents characterize at least most emotions; these constituents are commonly described as cognitive, motivational, and affective. Not just any combination of these elements constitutes an emotion, but arguably all are elements in any full-blooded emotion. They are understood differently by different writers on emotion[3] and need brief explanation.

[3] A great deal has been written on emotion, much of it confirming this tripartite conception (though our examples will illustrate cases in which at least the cognitive element may be, if not absent, then indefinite. Among the valuable book-length treatments are Robert M. Gordon, *The Structure of Emotions: Investigations in Cognitive Philosophy* (Cambridge: Cambridge University Press, 1987), Robert C. Solomon, *The Passions: Emotions and the Meaning of Life* (Indianapolis, IN: Hackett, 1993), Martha Nussbaum, *Upheavals of Thought: The Intelligence of Emotions* (Cambridge: Cambridge University Press, 2001), Roberts, *Emotions: An Essay in Aid of Moral Psychology*; and Linda Zagzebski,

The cognitive element in emotion need not be propositional; but even with objectual emotions, such as fearing a growling dog, there will normally be something believed about the object, say that it will bite one. Why only normally? We should allow that a tiny child who is not yet psychologically developed enough to form even attributive beliefs could be frightened of a growling dog. This fright might not be full-blooded fear, but fear it could be.[4] If being startled can be an emotion, and not (as may be more plausible) just a kind of shock akin to fear, it too has no cognitive component beyond what is required by the causative perception. In any case, cognitive content, for emotions having it, need not be carried by propositional beliefs, such as the belief *that the dog may bite me*. A disposition to *form* such beliefs might have to be present, but that is a different psychological property.

There is less controversy concerning whether emotions must have a motivational component. In experiencing an emotion, such

---

*Divine Motivation Theory* (Cambridge: Cambridge University Press, 2004). A recent short but wide-ranging treatment is Jon Elster's *Explaining Social Behavior: More Nuts and Bolts for the Social Sciences* (Cambridge: Cambridge University Press, 2007), esp. chap. 2, pp. 145–61. For him emotions "do not seem to form a *natural kind*" (146), which I find plausible. He goes on to list six features that are common and important, including triggering by beliefs (147). For reasons that will soon be apparent, I take many factors that evoke emotion to be pre-doxastic.

[4] Cf. John Deigh's view that any account of emotion must do justice to the fact that "emotions are common to both humans and beasts . . . [though] the set to which humans are liable is much greater than the set to which beasts are liable. . . ." He illustrates: "[T]he terror of horses fleeing a burning stable, the rage of a bull after provocation by a tormentor, and the delight of a hound in finding and retrieving its quarry are all examples." See his *Emotions, Values, and the Law* (Oxford: Oxford University Press, 2008), 18. On my view, these are not full-bloodedly emotions unless they embody beliefs. It is difficult to say whether animals might have the relevant kind of belief; certainly they may come close enough to have kinds of emotions at least very much like the same ones in human beings.

as fear, anger, or excitement, there will be something or other one wants, say to avoid the feared thing, to strike out at the object of anger, and to experience the exciting thing. Apathy, a sort of settled indifference, may seem to be an exception. But is apathy an emotion? If it is an emotion, and not the absence of emotion where one might expect it, apathy at least has a motivational *dimension*. That is, we expect no motivation where we realize it would otherwise be present. The person need not be indifferent to, say, what is genuinely frightening, but is not as easily excited and does not spontaneously feel such emotions as grief or nostalgia when, for normal persons, they are natural or even difficult to resist.

The affective dimension of emotion is roughly its feeling dimension—a phenomenal element that contrasts with the dispositional character of belief and motivation. Anger has a certain experiential feel; felt affection a quite different one; fear another still. Even apathy (which I include for comparison as significantly similar to certain emotions) might have a phenomenal element—a sense of impassivity or even of the unimportance of much in life. But whatever we say about the status of apathy, we can say that a person who cannot easily feel anything of the kind that goes with fear, anger, indignation, excitement, felt affection, disappointment, distress, and anxiety is unemotional; someone who easily feels these (or a similar range of emotions) might be considered emotional.

## The Intentionality and Judgmental Aspects of Emotion

Emotions are often regarded as intentional—to have intentionality as a kind of directedness toward their objects. This is chiefly because their objects are taken to be represented under some conceptualization. Consider first a propositional emotion: someone's being angry *that* Benito fired his secretary. This does not imply being angry that Benito fired the man who stole the petty cash, even if these are one and the same man. The angry person might have no inkling that the second, incriminating description applies to the secretary. Still—to move to a non-propositional emotion—fearing the growling dog *is* fearing the attacking pit bull terrier if they are one and the same. Like simple perceptions, objectual emotions—those with an external "direct object" such as a dog—can be truly ascribed using any correct description of their object. If someone fears the growling dog, which is Jake's pit bull, the person fears that pit bull, quite apart from having the concept of that species. The identity of that object, as opposed to the attributive content of the emotion (or perception)—say, that the dog has no leash, is not affected by the subject's intentionality.

We might also speak of attributive emotions, on analogy with attributive perceptions, where the emotion is toward a thing *as* taken to have a property. These emotions constitute an intermediate case, lying between simple emotions like fearing the pit bull and propositional ones like fearing that an accident will occur. I might see an approaching bear at nightfall as I take out recycling on a farm. Fearing such an approaching figure *as* threatening is possible without conceptualizing the figure, and certainly without verbally labeling it even subvocally, though not without a discriminative grasp of the property of being threatening (one sees it as, say, animalic, large, and approaching). But conceptualization is required by, say, fearing that *the bear* will attack. Even in the former, non-propositional case, however, the property of being threatening (and for me as for many others, the concept as well) figures in the intentional content of my emotion. Attributive emotions, then, are intentional, but not in the way propositional ones are. This point is easily missed if one views emotions as judgments. In that case, moreover—on the normal assumption that judgments have propositional objects—one should also be able to predicate truth or falsity of emotions.[5]

I have contended that, although emotions have an essential cognitive element, they are not in general properly considered true or false. But propositional objects are not the only elements that suffice for the intentionality of a psychological phenomenon. We may take emotions to be intentional because, at least typically, they embody *beliefs*, even if only attributive beliefs. Attributive beliefs exhibit intentionality. Believing a distant object, such as a bear, to be dangerous, for instance, does not entail believing it to have a significant likelihood of harming someone or doing damage, even if that is necessarily equivalent to being dangerous. The predicative contents of attributive beliefs are intentional objects in roughly the same way as the propositional objects of propositional beliefs.

---

[5] Here I depart from strong cognitive theories of emotion, those on which, as Roeser puts it, "emotions are judgments of value" (*Moral Emotions and Intuitions*, 202). Her view is, in part, that "emotions are states that are cognitive and affective . . . non-inferential, normative judgments. We can understand emotions as fulfilling the role of non-inferential judgments or intuitions . . . They bridge the is-ought gap and they let us make context-sensitive, holistic moral judgments. Paradigmatically, particular moral intuitions are emotions" (204). The judgmental view also encourages thinking of emotions as more behavioral than they are, at least insofar as judgments are *made*. But presumably a judgment can arise and be *held* without having been *made*, say in an episode of appraisal. Perhaps the judgment view is best understood as taking emotions to be *held* judgments, rather than *judgings* or their products. The truth-value problem and others remain, however. Further critical points bearing on the judgment view are made by Roberts, *Emotions: An Essay in Aid of Moral Psychology*, e.g. 87–89.

As our examples suggest, beliefs are paradigms of the cognitive element in emotions, even if that element might, in the convictional dimension, sometimes be weaker than belief, say a strong supposition (it might also be an intuitive seeming). With some emotions, such as fearing that the tornado will hit me, the belief or other cognitive element, such as an anticipation too weak to be belief, is propositional; but it is, in many emotions, attributive. An emotion may also embody beliefs of both kinds, such as fearing that the tornado will hit me and being terrified by the growing roar I believe to indicate its approaching.[6]

Desires (in the widest sense) are paradigms of the motivational element in emotion. Those elements may in any case be described as some kind of wanting. Love embodies a desire for the good of the person loved; envy typically embodies a desire for something (or a kind of thing) believed to belong to someone else (the object of envy); fear implies (typically) a desire that a felt danger be averted (or simply wanting the thing in question to change or disappear). What of free-floating anxiety? This can unsettle one, but its motivational power concerns more what one regards as relieving it than an object of worry—if it had a definite object, such as one's vulnerable child, it would not be free-floating.

It should be stressed, moreover, that there is no sharp distinction between certain aroused emotions and certain moods, such as sadness and agitation. Some cases of anxiety may be better

---

[6] Arguably, fearing that *p* is incompatible with believing that *p*, but the point might be pragmatic. If I believe *p*, it might be *odd* to say I fear that *p*, but must one stop fearing that the tornado will hit when one gains much evidence (and thereby believes) that it will? Perhaps in that case one passes into fearing *its impact*. In any case, anger illustrates the relevant point in the text: that an emotion can embody both kinds of belief. Anger with a man can be partly constituted by propositional belief that he did something nasty to his wife and believing him to be likely to continue the pattern.

classified as distressing moods rather than as emotions, and there are certainly borderline cases. To be sure, moods may have both affective and motivational constituents; but they are unlike emotions in not entailing beliefs or similar cognitive elements.

We have already seen cases which suggest that the affective element in emotion is more difficult to characterize than its cognitive and motivational elements. Perhaps we can say that this element is a matter of feeling; but different emotions are associated with different kinds of feeling, and of course non-occurrent emotions, such as anger with someone who is far from one's mind during one's tennis game, embody only dispositions to have feelings and do not entail presently experiencing any feeling. Consider the very different feelings that go with love versus hate, with fear versus delight, or with joy versus grief.

All emotions may exist in an occurrent form, since all can be elements present in—even dominant in—consciousness. But emotions may also exist dispositionally, as where they are possessed in the way love for one's family is when one is wholly occupied with some professional project and does not have them in mind. Might such cases as elation be exceptions? It may seem that whereas we can be angry with someone when the emotion is in no way present in consciousness, it is at least not obvious that, when our minds are wholly elsewhere, we can be elated about, say, a result of a project or revolted by someone's treatment of farm animals. But could someone not be elated about winning a lottery, even during hours when the person is concentrating on learning Italian? To be sure, we can call someone an angry person and leave it at that, implying that the person is either dispositionally or occurrently angry; but there is no comparable category of elated or delighted persons, and to call a person elated or delighted and leave it at that, with no qualifier, implies that the person is occurrently elated or delighted at the time of attribution. This, however, shows that some but not all emotion terms may have trait-ascriptive uses, not that emotions cannot be had dispositionally as well as occurrently.

In any case, to understand emotions, we must understand dispositional psychological properties. Possession of dispositional properties is more than a capacity to exhibit—given eliciting conditions—the kinds of events that count as manifestations of those properties. But possessing dispositional properties does not entail either a strong tendency to manifest them given those conditions, or even a definite probability of doing so given the conditions.[7] Consider resentment toward a coworker and an eliciting condition for that emotion, for instance someone's asking, privately, what one thinks of the person. There will be some tendency to make a negative judgment here; but the tendency may easily be inhibited by, for instance, discretion.

The relation between emotion and behavior manifesting it is typically indirect, and assigning a definite probability to any particular manifestation, such as damning with faint praise, is unlikely to be plausible. To be sure, we can usually count on certain eliciting conditions to cause an emotion possessed dispositionally to become occurrent, as where a close friend's question 'What do you think of him?' evokes felt resentment. But the emotion's becoming occurrent is not the only constitutive manifestation of the disposition, and it may be better called a realization of it.

[7] An account of the difference between dispositional beliefs and related phenomena, with much analysis concerning the constitution belief itself, is given in my "Dispositional Beliefs and Dispositions to Believe," cited in note 10 to Chapter 1.

*Intuition as a Cognitive Basis of Emotion*

Distinguishing between intuitions and emotions as we have does not require denying that the cognitive component of an emotion can be constituted by an intuition. Consider indignation again. If it seems to me, intuitively, that one person interviewing another is being unfairly inquisitive, that intuition may be the central cognition in both eliciting and sustaining my indignation toward the interviewer. I would be indignant toward the interviewer and would naturally explain this by saying that (e.g.) the questioning seems intrusive. An intuitive seeming might suffice; I need not actually believe that the interviewer is being intrusive. If this just intuitively seems so, that may suffice to arouse emotion. But certainly a doxastic intuition can also serve. This is not to imply that *only* intuitive cognitions can serve to evoke or sustain emotion. Another case is this: the unfairness may be so plain that one readily perceives, believes, and indeed knows that it is occurring. Here one may have not a moral intuition but simply a moral perception and perceptual moral knowledge. But intuition may guide our thought and emotion where the evidence does not yield knowledge or, sometimes, *before* it yields knowledge, judgment, or even simply belief.

Similar points hold for anger, which is next door to indignation, as the same example shows. What of resentment, which can be moral in content or at least morally based, as where it arises because of a moral judgment? Intuition, like perceptual belief and other cognitions, can serve as the cognitive component of emotion here too. But whereas the (correct) intuition that one person wronged another may justify indignation about the wrong even retrospectively, as where one vividly recalls an injustice, retrospective justification is less likely with resentment, at least when the resented party is disposed to make amends for the wrong. Suppose a correct intuition of wrongdoing justifies resentment initially, for instance where one of two business partners commits the firm to something major without consulting the other. It may cease to justify it when, because the bypassed partner should but does not see that generous reparation has been made by the other partner, the resentment remains. Resentment can persist after the offending party has made full reparations. This resentment outlives its justification.

Suppose, however, that the reparation cannot be ascertained by the resentful person, since it might be made anonymously. Then the person may remain justifiably resentful. But no matter how well justified one is in believing reparation was not made, one cannot know that it has not been made if in fact it has. As with belief, a justified emotion may yet be objectively groundless. This difference between justification and knowledge affects our assessment of emotion and not just our appraisal of beliefs. Some but not all emotions are, in their propositional forms, knowledge-entailing; many are factive; but few if any are constitutionally justified.

### Perceptually Based Intuitions and Emotional Responses

So far, the intuitions mentioned have not been viewed as the cognitive content of moral perceptions. But intuitive beliefs may arise *in* moral perceptions, as well as *with* them and *from* them. In all three cases, the kind of intuitive knowledge that perception can yield may produce a cognition central in an emotion in the ways we have illustrated for non-perceptual intuitions that figure in emotions. We might, for instance, hear intimidation in what one person says to another; and, through that perception and our sense of the vocabulary used, we might intuitively believe that the first is wronging the second and become angry that this is so. The sense of intimidating vocabulary, if properly grounded, can be an element in a moral perception whose basis is perception of properties that ground the wrongness of the act and whose cognitive content is an intuition. We may intuitively *see* that the one is wronging the other. That same intuition, under different conditions or in a different person, can be the cognitive component of a different emotion, say resentment. Seeing this wrong might then be the perceptual basis central in that moral emotion.

This is not to imply that *every* moral propositional perception has an intuition as its content. Consider seeing that by making a patently false allegation, someone is being unfair to a coworker. This (propositional) perception may be a clear case of moral knowledge based on conclusive evidence, and it is not a good candidate to be an intuition. That the first person is wronging the second is not *unintuitive*, but this kind of cognition is also not properly called an intuition. Even if the cognition is non-inferential, there is no exercise of *discernment*. Intuition is best understood as representing not a grasp of the obvious but rather a cognition of the kind that, often because a complex pattern is in view, can be the core of, or at least provide evidence for, judgment. With the perception of subtle intimidation, for instance, there is a need for discernment, and the intuition that the interviewer is intimidating the interviewee arises in the perception of the intimidation.

*With* this perception of intimidation, one may also have the intuition that the interviewer should not be allowed to continue.

*From* the perception, as one later considers aspects of the inter-viewee's response to the questions, one might (perhaps retrospectively) have the intuition that the interviewee is hurt. Similarly, seeing one person cheat another can yield the cognitive core of anger, say a judgment that the first was unjust to the second. The emotion of resentment can also arise with this perception; and from resentment of a certain acute kind one can become morally revolted by the cheater.

Intuitions and other cognitions may have causal as well as constitutive relations to emotions. A cognition that is central in an emotion and partly constitutive of it will not be at the time in question a cause of the emotion; but the cognition (say an in-tuition) might have earlier played a role in the formation of the emotion. An instructor's anger that a student cheated is partly constituted by believing that cheating is wrong and a betrayal of trust, even if that same belief did not cause (as opposed to being a necessary condition for) the anger of which it later became a part. It seems clear that any of the cognitive elements just described can give rise to emotion. They can cause it, and they can certainly sustain it. There is simply a change of role when such elements as intuiting, believing, or perceiving that an interviewer is being un-fair pass from causing indignation to being an element therein. A match that lights a fire can continue burning as part of the conflagration.

## II. The Evidential Role of Emotion in Moral Matters

An emotion can arise in response to properties that evidence the belief, or some belief, that is essential in the emotion. This has been illustrated with respect to indignation when it arises from intuiting unfairness in an interview. When the unfairness is so blatant as to be seen, we have a case where a moral perception, which entails moral knowledge or the possibility of it, can provide evidence for the judgment that the person in question is unfair. The same evidence may support such moral emotions as indignation and at least some kinds of resentment and guilt.

*Emotions as Rational Responses to Experience*

What evidential potentiality might an emotion, especially a moral one, have in its own right? This question arises mainly when the emotion does not emerge, as it commonly does, from an evidential cognition, one that either constitutes knowledge or is well-grounded and provides evidence for the emotion. In either of those quite common cases, that cognition gives the emotion an element of justification that enables it to provide, in turn, evidence for a moral judgment, such as that one person is being unfair to another. If I know that an essay was plagiarized, my anger that it was may partly justify a negative moral judgment of the plagiarizer derivatively from this knowledge. But here anger does little if any independent justificatory work. One might well have had, even without the emotion, the same degree of justification on the basis of a moral judgment, even if lesser motivation to act against the wrong than one has when anger fuels behavior. Emotion that embodies or responds to a moral judgment may better motivate appropriate action even where (as it may or may not do) it adds nothing to one's justification for that judgment.

To see how emotion can be evidential in its own right, apart from such a supportive cognition, consider indignation that

arises during an oral examination. Suppose I am judging a colleague who is conducting such an examination. I must rely on
my memory of the student's performance as well as on sensing
the nuances of the appraisal the colleague is apparently making.
Emotion, like perception and intuition, is often a response to a
pattern, and it may be quite rational in the light of that pattern.
Perhaps in such cases emotion often responds to the whole as
more than the sum of the parts. The content and style of an oral
examination or an interview, for instance, may globally *ill-befit*
the level of competence that one can expect in the kind of student
or interviewee under examination. This unfittingness may be apparent during the oral examination, as one watches the individu-
ally difficult though acceptable challenges and sees the pained ex-
pressions of the candidate struggling to reply. There may also be
an unfittingness of the colleague's descriptions of what the candidate said. They may, for instance, be too harsh by exaggerating or
ridiculing the candidate's mistakes. My indignation, arising from
a sense of an examiner's demandingness as ill-befitting the low
level of the student, may be part of my basis for thinking that the
examiner has been unfair to the student.

   It will help here to consider a quite different emotion, anxiety, which is not a moral emotion. I was once temporarily hosted
by someone I had only just met. He was acting in a disturbingly
strange way. We were sitting alone in a dining area where several kitchen knives lay on the table at which I was lunching. He
stared at them for a time and was silent while doing so, though
the conversation resumed. I found myself uncomfortable. I had
no belief that he might be dangerous or even that he was seriously disturbed, and I do not think that I drew any inference
from anything I believed concerning his psychological makeup.

This is not to say that I could not have formed beliefs that would be a basis for having the emotion I had begun to feel. But I later saw that my anxiety—which was likely a response to many more indications than his staring at the knives—was some evidence of his being seriously disturbed. (Later incidents unmistakably confirmed that he was indeed disturbed that day.)

In this kind of case, although the emotion does not embody an intuition or a cognition that evidences a judgment, the emotion itself may play an evidential role in supporting such cognitions. It may be a perfectly rational response to a pattern that may at least temporarily evade description.[8] In this and similar kinds of cases, moral emotion (among other emotions) may be quite analogous to certain kinds of aesthetic responses. It may also lead to and supplement moral judgment. Suppose an empathic friend felt anxious for me in the lunch setting in which my host is acting strangely. This could lead to judging that I should not be left alone with him.

In part because it may be a rational response to what is perceived, a moral emotion may support a moral intuition, such as that one person is being unfair to another. It may also support a

[8] Compare this with the strong view that "since moral judgments depend, at bottom, on how we respond emotionally to the world around us, the idea of a *purely* rational approach to morality is an oxymoron. To be sure, the idea of a purely emotional approach to morality would also be a contradiction in terms; to engage in moral deliberation is to step back from one's immediate reaction and think critically about it." See Gregory E. Kaebnick, "Reasons of the Heart: Emotion, Rationality, and the 'Wisdom of Repugnance,'" *The Hastings Center Report* 38, no. 4 (2008): 36–45, 36. My position does not require dependence of all moral judgments on emotion, nor would I contrast the emotional with the rational in the way suggested here, but Kaebnick's paper does provide useful examples of the way emotional responses may have evidential weight. For another contrast with Kaebnick's view, see Catherine Z. Elgin, *Considered Judgment* (Princeton, NJ: Princeton University Press, 1996).

non-moral response, such as a belief that a person is disturbed. Those intuitions in turn may evidentially support moral judgments. For some judgments, moral as well as non-moral, an emotion may be the primary support, at least initially. In other cases the emotion may be a response to an intuition or other cognition that is itself evidence, or intuition and emotion may be common responses to the same evidencing factors, as where a moral perception of intimidation yields both.

## An Evolutionary Speculation

One may naturally speculate here that there is an evolutionary explanation for the evidential value of emotion. Emotions often motivate appropriate behavior, and their arising in situations of some danger might have survival value. Take fear. Because it is highly motivating and can rapidly produce avoidance behavior, it can play a protective role which a belief that there is danger cannot as readily play. The belief must evoke motivation before it can yield self-protective action; the fear has motivation as a constituent. If fear is sufficiently often warranted by the sense of danger or threats that evoke that sense—and we know that it not infrequently is often warranted—its role in producing rapid defensive responses might be expected to give it fitness value.

Liking—as felt attraction for another—provides a different example. If courting behavior always had to wait upon the formation of approving beliefs about the object of pursuit, human life would be quite different. This is not just because such beliefs—say, to the effect that the person has good character—typically do not motivate as well as does positive emotion; it is also because many relationships would not come into being at all if they were not initially fueled by a warm glow. Delight may come faster than approval, approval more readily than sober judgment. On the aversive side, then, the survival value of fear as part of a warning system is clear, and similar points hold for other "negative" emotions. The survival value of the "positive" emotions is connected not just with their capacity to facilitate mating, but with their capacity to support cooperative behavior.[9]

If emotions might have a kind of fitness value in part because of their ability to evidence such phenomena as danger—whether from natural forces or from the machinations of other people—we might wonder whether they may have a kind of *evidential autonomy*. In particular, are there kinds of facts which, apart from emotional evidence, one could not have evidence for or, especially, know? I cannot see that in principle there are facts that can be evidenced or known *only* by emotions or emotional elements. For one thing, emotions themselves are in large part responses to perceived phenomena, such as the behavior of others, or at least experienced elements such as anxiety or envisaging events. It would appear that in principle, at least, the evidential aspects of these phenomena, whether external or internal, can be captured by propositions that can be known or justifiedly believed, or by predications that can be known or justifiedly accepted, apart from emotion. Suppose this is so. Assume, for instance, that one person's being unfair to another can be known

---

[9] There is much literature concerning how, from a neurobiological point of view, emotions might conduce to survival; see, e.g., Thagard and Finn, "Conscience: What Is Moral Intuition?"; Jorge Mall, Ricardo De Oliveira-Souza, and Roland Zahn, "Neuroscience and Morality: Moral Judgments, Sentiments, and Values," in Narvaez and Lapsley, *Personality, Identity, and Character*, 106–35; and, for a developmental perspective, Darcia Narvaez, "Triune Ethics Theory and Moral Personality," in Narvaez and Lapsley, *Personality, Identity, and Character*, 136–58.

through a cognitive grasp of the actions of the former toward the latter, their manner of performance, and their motivation. It does not follow that, *given* our natural constitution, we in fact can know such unfairness to occur without emotional discernment.

————

The importance of emotional evidence in ethical matters is great and is best appreciated when its relation to moral perception on one side and, on another side, moral intuition is taken into account. Even if all knowable moral truths could be known apart from emotional evidence—and I do not claim this—we might well know many of them much less readily if we had to learn them through forming beliefs carrying sufficient evidential information that is independent of emotion. The reasonable conclusion to draw here is that it is not only possible that, through the evidence of emotion, often where the emotion is connected with intuition, we sometimes know things we would not otherwise know. We also know some things more *readily* through that evidence than we would have if our knowledge depended on non-emotional evidence. This point may often hold even where, apart from emotional discernment, we would have discovered the same things. The importance of emotion in the moral domain will become still more apparent as we consider a wider range of moral judgments.

# CHAPTER 7

# The Place of Emotion and Moral Intuition in Normative Ethics

WE NOW HAVE BEFORE US the core of a theory of moral perception and its relation to both intuition and emotion. Many examples have been provided to illustrate all three of these interrelated notions and support a view of their importance in ethics and elsewhere. The theory can be further supported and clarified, however, by considering all three in relation to the kinds of moral judgments central for practical ethics. This will require further discussion of both emotion and intuition, an illustration of how they arise in several moral domains, and a sketch of the place of moral imagination in bringing both to bear on the formation of moral judgments.

## I. EMOTION AND MORAL INTUITION

Emotion may issue in and support intuition by responding to a pattern of factors. This may occur in at least three ways. Take indignation produced by witnessing subtly exploitive conduct.

First, witnessing (hence perceiving) that conduct can directly produce indignation whose character, say as highlighting wrongdoing, supports an intuition of injustice. In a second kind of case, emotion may indirectly affect intuition, causally and evidentially. It may, for instance, lead to reflection that evokes and has content that supports intuition, as where one is surprised to find oneself annoyed with someone, reflects on why one is annoyed, discerns reasons for this, and, on the basis of this pattern of factors, has an intuition that the person's manner of speaking to one is slightly patronizing. The intuition may arise here as a kind of conclusion of reflection, as opposed to a conclusion of inference. It may be a phenomenal seeming and in some cases may pass into a confident intuitive belief.

In a third kind of case, which may initially resemble the second kind, an emotion may yield premises from which we infer a proposition. Here we arrive at a conclusion of inference. This proposition may or may not be one that, in the circumstances, we might have inferred apart from the role of emotion in providing us with pertinent information. Recall my anxiety in the awkward kitchen scene. By contrast with the case as presented earlier—as directly giving rise to an intuition that something is wrong with my companion—I could have simply thought that he looked at the knives too long, that he seemed nervous, and that he became strangely distant from me in the conversation. These indications support the proposition that he is disturbed, and one might infer that from them. But they may also arouse an emotion such as anxiety directly, rather than through producing cognitions that elicit and propositionally justify it; and reflection on the emotion, say on how one is feeling and toward what, might non-inferentially yield the same belief one might have arrived inferentially.

It should be no surprise that emotion can support intuition and its propositional content in the ways I have described. Emotion is often a discriminative response to perceptible aspects of people or of things in our environment. In some cases it can magnify, unify, or extend the work of perception and thereby provide evidence concerning the person or situation perceived. The evidence may derive its force largely from the perceptible elements that underlie emotion, but emotion may also provide a kind of evidence of its own. It may reliably indicate significant truths about people or situations even if its doing so depends on indications that in principle can be ascertained in some other way.

## *Can Moral Emotions Discriminate among Kinds of Obligations?*

In the cases of emotional response just described—where emotion responds to experiencing patronizing conduct and to strange behavior—intuition also emerges. But this is other-directed intuition, whose content concerns others' conduct; its content does not express felt obligation on the part of its possessor. Might moral emotion generate or support this latter kind of cognition, as intuition can? To be sure, moral emotion can be evidentially important even if its range in discriminatively responding to moral phenomena is narrower than that of intuition. It is narrower, since intuitions are as diverse as the huge and virtually unlimited range of propositions constituting their contents, and there are surely more propositions having moral significance than there are distinct moral emotions. But in absolute terms, the range of moral emotions is not narrow.

A good way to see the breadth and importance of emotions in ethics is to consider W. D. Ross's eight principles of prima facie obligation, which are plausibly regarded as expressing at least a large proportion of our basic moral obligations.[1] With those principles in view, we can explore the kinds of emotions appropriate to observing violation or fulfillment of the obligations in question. This is not to suggest that for *every* type of obligation there is a distinctive kind of emotion. That seems doubtful, but it may well be that, for every *basic* kind of moral obligation, there is a distinct kind of emotion, or a range of types of emotion, befitting to it.

The eight prima facie obligations posited by Ross's principles are quite comprehensive. All of them may be associated with moral emotions that, in widely varying circumstances, can evidence violation of the obligations that the principles designate or conformity with what the principles require. In this way, emotions may play a major role in morally important conduct and are an important topic in normative ethics. In illustrating the kinds of emotion that may be appropriate to them, we can also clarify the range of phenomenal elements befitting moral perceptions with similar content. Those phenomenal elements alone do not individuate the perceptions or fully account for their befitting the moral situations in question, but the phenomenal elements in moral perception and in associated emotions may play both evidential and motivational roles.

---

[1] See chap. 2 of *The Right and the Good* for Ross's introduction and most influential discussion of these principles. In chap. 5 of *The Good in the Right* I discuss them further and introduce refinements and some revisions of Ross's formulations.

*1. Justice.* This is the obligation to treat people in accord with their merit (merit is the notion Ross stressed, though he also had in mind such notions as equal treatment and desert). Consider someone with a sense of justice who sees disproportionate distributions, say in people's grading papers or apportioning food to the needy after a flood. Such a person is likely to exhibit a negative feeling of unfittingness, or an unsettling sense of discord, or a disturbing feeling of imbalance. Here emotion evidences injustice. On the positive side, justice may also be perceived and may be indicated by emotion. There is, for instance, a sense of satisfaction in giving grades that genuinely reflect actual examination scores and seminar performance marks. Moreover, sometimes one does not settle on a difficult distribution *until* such an emotion arises. It may play a confirmatory or a disconfirmatory role, and its success in either case may later be verified by the review and by further information possible with the passage of time. Felt unfittingness in a projected distribution, such as a set of grades, may produce anxiety. The sense of justice may replace anxiety by relief. In cases like these, emotion, when suitably responsive to morally relevant elements, can be evidence for justice as well as for injustice.

*2. Non-injury.* A second obligation Ross noted is non-injury: the obligation not to injure or harm people. We may experience moral revulsion or outrage on seeing a man lash a child for spilling milk, or slap his wife for smiling at a friendly waiter who greets them as they reach their table. Such violence, especially when self-defense is not in evidence, is repelling in a way that is moral and readily evokes disapproval. There may be shock, but there is also the kind of negative response that makes criticism natural and energizes defensive or punitive treatment. Injury and harm may also produce other negative emotions. Film footage of genocidal slaughter may evoke moral outrage.

***3. Veracity.*** The obligation in question is not to lie—to be truthful in speaking (as opposed to simply speaking truly).[2] The emotion of indignation may arise on hearing a lying accusation about a coworker, told to the worker's supervisor. Again, moral emotion may contribute to the phenomenal element in moral perception; and for moral emotion as for intuition, the sense of unfittingness can be a main basis. The unfittingness of saying that *p* when *p* is perceptibly false is a clear case. Thought and imagination may work much as perception does in such matters. Envisaged action, as well as perceived action, may also evoke emotion; and here the power and vividness of a person's moral imagination is especially important. People who have internalized the principle of veracity may feel emotion *prospectively*, as where a perceived or imagined temptation to lie evokes revulsion. That revulsion may in turn produce a negative judgment opposing the lie. Internalization of other moral standards may yield the same kind of sensitivity. On the positive side, the prospect of resisting a temptation to lie can give one a feeling of relief of tension or a sense of gratification. There may be no ordinary name for the kind of emotion in question. Emotions are more various than our names for them; but there is a kind of positive feeling that can accompany such moral perceptions and moral imaginings, and they may be positively motivating in a way that supports moral conduct.

[2] Two clarifications will help. First, saying something true need not constitute being truthful; the statement may be intentionally misleading or accidentally made. Second, veracity—roughly honesty—may be mistakenly conceived as the disposition to communicate truth when a circumstance or question—say, 'Do you believe *p*?'—makes that relevant. It is not quite equivalent to that and withholding truth even when asked one's beliefs need not count against veracity. Some people should be put off or greeted with silence. Taciturnity does not imply dishonesty. What counts against veracity is chiefly lying, as well as certain kinds of deception. *Some* tendency to cooperate with certain inquirers may be a requirement of veracity *as a virtue*; but to explicate all that would require an excursion into the theory of veracity.

**4. Promissory Fidelity.** This is the obligation to keep promises. Seeing someone breaking a promise to help a friend's child—say, self-ishly spending the money given for this purpose—may arouse anger, disgust, or, where the offense is not grievous, moral disappoint-ment or a disapproving sense of the deed's ill-befitting the promis-sory words. These emotions may occur together or sequentially, and may be mingled with still other emotional responses or with moral judgments. Experiencing promises broken toward oneself may evoke emotion even more readily, and here much depends on one's relation to the other. One might be furious with a child who breaks a promise that causes suspension from school, hurt by a friend who abandons a joint project, and downcast when a patient who had promised absti-nence reverts to drinking. In some of these cases, as with abandon-ment of joint projects, it may be the character of the emotion, say its element of disapprobative resentment, that makes clear to us that the conduct is *morally* wrong. Indignation is another emotion some-times appropriate to breach of promise, particularly where there is evidently no mitigating factor. The emotion may be focused on the combination of the broken promise and the absence of any excuse; the sense of discord between deed and circumstance may here be part of the phenomenology.

**5. Beneficence.** Beneficence is the obligation to do good deeds, for instance in reducing the suffering, or enhancing the well-being, of others. Take the negative case first—failure to fulfill this obligation. Imagine the anger and distress of witnessing, when one has no phone, someone's refusal even to call for help when an injured and bleeding accident victim requests it and the only explanation is the hurry of the person who, with a cell phone in evidence, rushes away. Such eva-sive conduct ill-befits the victim's salient need. If the injury is serious and the victim dies, one might have an acute sense of loss and distress, perhaps mingled with indignation. If the injury is not serious, it may evoke not indignation or even anger, but only an empathic sense of frustration. By contrast, imagine someone who risks danger to save a drowning person. There are such emotions as moral admiration and a kind of pride in certain voluntary good deeds. We might feel like applauding as the swimmer pulls the victim to safety.

*6. Self-improvement.* This is the obligation to improve one's character or knowledge. It is perhaps less likely to be evidenced by emotion, in part because it is self-directed and its fulfillment is often laborious, so that non-fulfillment is commonly mitigated by one's legitimate reasons to expend energy elsewhere. But we can be angry with ourselves for failures, and if they are moral we can feel a kind of distress; we can also feel gratified or even delighted if we sense improvement in developing some capacity we view as important in treating others as we ought to. Here we might also think of parents who discover the children playing a video game instead of doing their homework or practicing their instruments. Even where the children have broken no promise, a parent may have a sense of their abandoning what should be their values. A likely emotion is a keenly felt combination of disappointment and disapproval.

*7. Reparation.* Roughly, this is the obligation to make amends for harms or injuries to others. Imagine seeing someone who, while borrowing a computer to do an e-mail, loses a friend's unsaved file filled with data and then does nothing—barely saying 'sorry' and then leaving the scene. Here one might easily feel moral annoyance, even resentment. The friend has been "used" in a way that approaches what Kant called treatment of a person "merely as a means." Empathy may facilitate such responses, but it is not required for one. Here as with other obligations, empathy may be manifested in reflected emotion. I feel the abuse of my friend and am resentful somewhat as if I were abused. A parent may feel embarrassment for a son who is himself embarrassed at failing to reconstruct a toy he has broken.

**8. *Gratitude.*** Roughly, the obligation of gratitude is to reciprocate, or at least to express appreciation, for good deeds toward us.[3] Consider someone who accepts help with a flat tire and, after the polite young man helping completes the hard work and soils his clothes, does not even thank him, saying only 'I'm glad that's over'. This is an occasion for sharp disapproval, likely felt keenly. Anger might also be natural. A mere acknowledgment of the successful work ill-befits the man's generosity and sacrifice that call for gratitude. The unfittingness here parallels that illustrated by failure of reparation. Failure in reparation ill-befits one's own bad-doing; failure in gratitude ill-befits someone else's good-doing.

In earlier work I have proposed adding to Ross's list prima facie obligations of two other kinds: obligations to preserve and enhance *liberty* (roughly, to preserve and advance freedom in human conduct) and those of *respectfulness* (obligations to do *what* one is obligated to do, in an appropriate *way*, understood in terms of the *manner* of action as opposed to its *matter*, its type).[4] Here too moral emotion may be revealing and may produce in-

---

[3] Cf. Ross: "I use 'gratitude' to mean returning of services" (*The Right and the Good*, 23). Even apart from not applying to the attitudinal use of the term, this suggests that gratitude requires reciprocity that goes beyond expression of appreciation. Reciprocity, especially in kind or at the same level, is only one way to manifest gratitude. For discussion of its scope, see chap. 5 of *The Good in the Right*.

[4] These two prima facie obligations are introduced and discussed in some detail in chap. 5 of *The Good in the Right*.

tuition or judgment or both (though in different circumstances they may produce emotions). Let us consider these obligations in turn.

Regarding the obligation of liberty, consider the natural feeling of relief from moral distress, sometimes combined with a sense of moral satisfaction, when someone innocent of a crime is set free. Similarly, when we see someone unduly restricted, as where authorities prevent a person with a minority view from speaking in a meeting, we may have a sense of oppression, or at least feel an empathic distress. It is true that the sense of justice is also a possible source of emotion there, but justice need not be involved. An unwarranted restraint, even where it is within the rights of the chair of a meeting, is enough to evoke a sense of violating an obligation to respect freedom. As this suggests, our sense of the value of liberty may be manifested even where no moral right is threatened. Imagine someone who, out of irrational fear, cannot fly in a plane. One ought to help here if one can. We might feel both grateful and relieved at the good done as we watch friends patiently dispel the unfounded fears and liberate the person for flying.

With obligations of manner, a multitude of emotions may occur. This is in good part because the adverbial properties in question (typically expressed by descriptive terms ending in *ly*) are multifarious, often salient, and higher order, presupposing the act-properties they modify and often bringing home to a perceiver the distinctive manner, style, or unique character of an action. We may thus be indignant at the right deed's being *cruelly* done, and we may be annoyed at a potentially fine gesture of reparation made *clumsily*, or a positive evaluation given *patronizingly*. Annoyance might overshadow the moral satisfaction we might otherwise feel, or the two emotions might mingle to yield something quite unusual. Emotion is even more likely to be aroused when something hurtful to a person is done in a wrongful way. Arresting offending teenagers may be necessary when they have damaged a library; but, when they are cooperating, they should not be arrested *violently*, say shoved into a van or spoken to in a racially or ethnically insulting way. The sight of either immoral way of making the arrest will tend to arouse negative emotions in sensitive impartial witnesses.

### Internal and External Modes of Emotional Support

Emotions can be evidential for intuitions and judgments in many ways. Some are internal, others external. Let me explain these in turn.

When an intuition that an emotion supports is based on and colored by the experience that both generates the emotion and provides a rational basis for that emotion, the emotion supports the intuition in an internal way. Imagine a physician who considers ordering force-feeding for a dying patient in our care. An emotional revulsion to the envisaged prospect, whether this revulsion arises before or simultaneously with an intuitive judgment that the force-feeding is wrong, may support that judgment. The vivid thought of the manipulated helpless patient may produce both an emotional revulsion and an intuitive sense—or an intuitive belief or intuitive judgment—that the deed would be wrong. The rational and sustaining basis of the emotion is an element that is central for the justification of the intuition (or other cognition). The emotional revulsion and the distressing intuition are unified as responses to the same perceptions and thoughts.

In a way, they may be mutually reinforcing. Each is a response to the same pattern that justifies the negative judgment, and the emotion contributes to the phenomenal element in the intuition. In this way, emotion can enhance an intuition's strength, clarity, and justificatory force.

A second way emotion may internally support an intuition is also suggested by some of our examples. The emotion may not only confirm the presence of properties that support the content of an intuition; it may also *magnify* evidence supporting that content. In the force-feeding case, magnification may enhance internal support. The contours of such deeds as deceiving and intimidating can also be highlighted by an emotional response to them. Here what is more brightly displayed is likely to be more readily appraised.

A third way emotions may internally support intuitions is as follows. An *aspect* of emotion, such as the negative feeling that goes with moral revulsion, may also figure in the intuition itself, which may be to the effect that one person was unjust to another. When there is internal evidential support of the intuition by the emotion, this is largely a matter of the emotion's indicating the property (or a property) that the intuition centrally represents, say being unjustly intrusive. Recall the indignation one may feel toward an unfair interviewer. This may be a discriminative response to the wrong-making element(s) that evoke that emotion, and the negatively felt sense of, say, violation of privacy may support the negative intuition that the act is wrong. The negative, disapprobative aspect of the emotion, focused as it is on those elements, supports the intuition of wrongdoing.

An emotion can also externally support an intuition, belief, or judgment. This occurs when it operates as an element in a moral deliberative process undertaken where moral judgment and action are required. It may also occur when emotion is a response to an abstract scenario, as where, in a seminar, we consider thought experiments. The same intuition of wrongness in ordering force-feeding could be based on my reflection on the artificiality of sustaining life in that situation by those invasive means. Now suppose I then note that my emotional reaction is also negative and, if I am not skeptical about the value of emotional responses, I may take this to be confirmatory. One might think: why would I feel upset at the prospect of the force-feeding if it were really an acceptable option? Why can't I reconcile myself to it? Here what is crucial is that—at least for a person of self-trust or belief in emotions as sometimes indicative of the character of their objects—the emotion itself has evidential value. My taking appropriate account of the emotion itself, and not its basis or its effect on some element in intuition, is what plays the confirmatory role. That role may be non-inferential, as where I simply form an intuition in response to the pattern of which the emotion is a confirmatory part. It may also be inferential, as where the fact that I have the emotion provides a premise for a judgment that seems indicated by its presence or character.

Broadly speaking, then, where an emotion externally supports an intuition, the support is by way of the person's taking account of that emotion, with the emotion or some aspect of it operating as a datum that confirms the propositional content of the intuition and may be cited in support of that proposition. By contrast, emotions internally support intuitions when both are non-inferential responses to the same phenomena and the character of the intuition is affected by the emotion in a way that enhances its credibility in relation to the evidential facts that support both. Where the external support provided by an emotion yields a belief or judgment, that support may be inferential, with a premise concerning the emotion (or some aspect of it) playing a major role. An intuitive response with the same content, by contrast, is cognitive, but non-inferential; and in contrast to all of those cases (and other cognitive cases) the emotional response has affective and motivational elements as well, and their presence, as responding discriminatively to the same phenomena, may both support the intuition or other cognitive element and motivate behavior appropriate to that cognition.

None of this implies that all emotions must confirm some intuition. Emotions may profoundly mislead, and some occur with no connection to the person's intuitions or other cognitions, such as judgments. But emotions are often rational and, contrary to one stereotype, they need not tend to falsify the beliefs they engender or help to sustain.

An interesting and difficult question that arises here is whether, if one accurately observed a situation that would ordinarily arouse emotion—say one person's patronizing another by "talking down" to the other—one might then form beliefs which yield premises that, at least as well as the emotion of indignation, support the intuition that (for instance) the patronizing person is being unfair to the other. This case is possible in principle. It is the facts that ultimately evidence singular moral judgment. Whether we respond to them emotionally or intuitively does not change this. It might happen, however, that for some people the direct route from emotion to moral intuition or moral judgment is more natural than the inferential route from beliefs expressing the relevant perceived facts to the judgment. There may be other people for whom that direct route is rarely traversed or often closed.[5]

[5] The distinction between internal and external roles of emotions in supporting moral judgment may be clarified by considering the roles that—despite

The capacities in question may vary independently: some people are more emotionally sensitive or more intuitive than others, though a person might be emotionally sensitive yet not particularly intuitive, or intuitive but not particularly emotional. People also differ in the extent to which their moral beliefs and judgments arise from evidential beliefs as opposed to perceptual or emotional responses to the evidencing facts themselves. It must also be kept in mind that overdetermination is possible: an emotion can directly support an intuition at the same time one realizes facts—which may or may not be bases of the emotion—that also support it.

## II. Moral Imagination as a Nexus of Intuition, Emotion, and Perception

Most of our examples of emotions as responses to experience have been cases in which perception plays a crucial causative role. This range of examples is appropriate given our concern with moral perception. But the importance and pervasiveness of perceptual experiences that give rise to emotion must not be allowed to obscure the point that emotion and intuition can arise from imaginative experience and can indeed provide evidence for moral judgments in those cases as well as where emotion arises from actual perception. Such imaginative experience can manifest what is sometimes called *moral imagination*. The term 'moral imagination' is not to be construed in the most natural way, on

common interpretations of Kant—emotions can play in Kantian ethics. Here Carla Bagnoli's "Emotions and the Categorical Authority of Moral Reasons" (in her *Morality and the Emotions*, 62–81), which explores Kant's resources for taking account of emotions in ethics, is instructive. She treats respect, e.g., as the "emotional aspect of practical reason." See esp. 75–78.

analogy with 'moral person', 'moral virtue', or 'moral character'. That construal yields a contrast with non-moral imagination, and this is not central for the notion of moral imagination. That notion is not a concept of a *kind* of imagination, but rather of imagination *in* the moral sphere.

Deliberation and moral judgment may be assisted by imaginative representation of the kinds of situation in question. We can sometimes be as emotionally sensitive, or as intuitively insightful, when we imagine a situation calling for decision as when we actually see one person relating to another in an actual situation of just that kind. Much as memory can preserve what we have perceived in situations of certain kinds, imagination can outline what we *would* perceive in situations of those kinds.

By contrast with perception, imagination is creative. Perception fails us if it is not faithful to its object; it is properly limited by facts. Imagination fails us if it does not transcend its starting points; it is properly limited by (at most) possibilities. Imagination apparently depends on the world, or at least on experience, for raw material; but it can build indefinitely many structures from that material, whereas perception is more a reproductive than a constructive faculty. Both are representational, but perception depends on the object perceived, whereas imagination can manipulate the objects it represents—whether spontaneously or in accordance with our will. Perception is tied to its objects; imagination, even if it requires raw material from perception, is limitlessly combinatory, often dynamic, and readily responsive to our desire for even minute alteration.

In the moral realm, imagination can construct morally significant scenarios we have never experienced. This is perhaps the most common kind of exercise of moral imagination, and it greatly aids prospective deliberation about what to do. But it may also bring to the evaluation of past deeds, whether by ourselves or by others, alternatives we have experienced in other situations. We may wonder why, in a difficult matter, we did not do what succeeded elsewhere or why friends who failed in an attempt to do right did not do what they themselves should have observed their mentors doing. Such reflection is capable of great subtlety if it is aided not just by memories of relevant experiences but also by imagining possible alternatives.

If moral imagination can take us far beyond what we have perceived, it also tends (with the help of memory) to preserve that and to use it—or elements in a perception—in facilitating judgment. One case is this: if we have seen a kind of wrongdoing, then imagining a case significantly similar to it may well tend to evoke moral disapproval (an attitude), a sense of wrongdoing (a phenomenal response), or even an intuition that the imagined deed is wrong (a cognition). It may also evoke the emotion of indignation, which may well befit the case. The more closely the imagination "brings back" the perceived wrongdoing (or right-doing), the more reasonable it is to expect moral emotion or a moral cognition, whether intuitive or doxastic, with similar content.

The path between moral perception and moral imagination is not, however, a one-way street, with perception always playing the generative role. Consider how we often imaginatively create a situation of action in order to decide what to do in a similar one, or imaginatively create a scenario to fill out moral narratives we read or hear, as where a friend sketchily describes ill-treatment. Such exercises of imagination can heighten our perceptual sensitivity. If we imagine how we would regard a kind of treatment by someone, whether we are hoping for it, fearing it, or simply envisaging it, then we may be more likely to perceive such treatment if it occurs. Moreover, if moral intuition is evoked by what we imagine, might this not increase the likelihood of our having moral perceptions with a similar content when confronted with a case resembling the imagined one? These hypotheses are empirical and seem quite worth exploring scientifically. I cannot claim to know that they hold. What is evident given the reflections before us, however, is significant: perception can supply the imagination with both raw materials and cognitive inclinations, and imaginative activity in which they figure, especially when integrated with emotional responses to its objects, can heighten our perceptual sensitivity to phenomena of similar content.

It seems beyond doubt that imagination exercised in the moral sphere can yield intuition. Intuition, in turn, can produce emotion, which, in ways we have seen, can support moral judgment. Moral imagination can also yield emotion directly. Whether or not moral imagination produces intuition, emotion, or moral judgment, and in what order, is variable; and how each of these three is related to the others in a given case is a contingent matter. The point is that moral imagination, like moral perception, can yield and support intuition, emotion, and moral judgment. This is perhaps to be expected: the exercise of moral imagination can, through vivid imaging of morally significant events, and through envisaging diverse possibilities, produce an experience significantly like a moral perception.

Some people have more imagination than others. This tends to make them more intuitive and more susceptible to moral emotion. But the connection between imagination and, on the other hand, intuition and emotion is not tight. Someone could be imaginative in moral matters, but not especially intuitive therein and not unusual in emotional sensitivity in moral matters. It also seems possible to have clear and reliable intuitions, in moral or other matters, even without being imaginative, or to be emotionally sensitive without being imaginative. One would think that being highly discriminating perceptually, at least where this occurs in the moral realm, would tend to stimulate moral imagination; but even if there is such a tendency, we may find only a contingent and variable connection. Moral imagination, then, can provide evidence and can do so in a way that parallels the way moral perception provides it. Whether, in a given person, either moral emotion or moral perception plays a large role in moral life depends on many variables. The development of moral emotion and moral perception at a high level is surely a mark of good moral education and cultural maturity.

## III. Intuition and Moral Judgment

So far, I have considered intuitions and other cognitions and their relation to emotion, but I have not focused specifically on judgment. The notion of moral judgment is among the central concepts in ethics. I refer to two related elements: one is *judging*; the other is judgment as the cognition one retains when one judges that *p* (some proposition) and then *holds* the judgment dispositionally. This retention of judgment is common where we make a judgment on which no action is needed at the time, and we retain the judgment either spontaneously or with the idea of (for instance) following or expressing it later.

One might wonder why judgment, as opposed to belief with the same propositional content, is so important. It is, after all, beliefs that are the basic cognitions we act on (desire is crucial for action, too, but I leave it aside for now since desire is conative, not cognitive, and raises question that cannot be pursued here).[6] One reason for the importance of judgment is that judgment that *p*—in the sense of 'judging' that *p*—can invest the belief that *p* with both sharper focus and additional power to yield inference or action on the basis of *p*. We must at least briefly entertain or focus on what we judge. Moreover, the natural occasions for judgment commonly invite, and often demand, reflection; but we need not even think of, much less focus on, consider, or entertain, all the propositions we believe. For many kinds of propositions we believe, and even for many we act on, we do not consider or even entertain them.

Testimony and perception provide two major sources of examples that illustrate the contrast between judging that *p* and merely believing it. When friends tell me about the sights and sounds on their recent trip, I form beliefs as naturally and quickly as they express them. I typically do not consider the propositions they affirm; and I can believe what they tell me as quickly as I hear it and without focusing on it. If I immediately accept *p*, *q*, and *r* as a friend affirms them in a narrative, I will have the passing *thoughts*, that *p*, *q*, and *r*; but this does not require entertaining or even focusing on those propositions. Entertaining a proposition, as is common with judging, is focal and goes beyond simply having the thought of the proposition. A different kind of example concerns cases in which one forms beliefs upon making observa-

---

[6] In chaps. 3–6 of *The Architecture of Reason: The Structure and Substance of Rationality* (Oxford: Oxford University Press, 2001) I have extensively discussed what constitutes rational desire. Further analysis is provided in my "Prospects for a Naturalization of Practical Reason: Humean Instrumentalism and the Normative Authority of Desire," *International Journal of Philosophical Studies* 10, no. 3 (2002): 235–63.

tions (and there are other cases). When I check the tool closet for bolts, I form beliefs about their sizes and number as I observe the supply; I need do nothing that is plausibly viewed as thinking of or, especially, considering the propositions I come to know.

This difference between judgment and belief is one factor that makes judgment more subject to critical reflection or filtering out than belief in general. For considering or even just focusing on a proposition, especially if it is complex, tends to give us a better grasp of it than simply coming to believe it as someone asserts it or as, in casual circumstances, we observe that it holds. Indeed, typically, we have no occasion to make judgments unless we see some need to consider some matter. This typical background of the making of a judgment contributes to its special role in our understanding of cognition and action. The judgments people make tell us something about them that we do not learn simply from knowing that they hold the beliefs those judgments express—which is not to say that we cannot learn much about people from knowing some of the beliefs they hold that were not formed through making judgments with the same propositional content. As to action, what we do on the basis of judgment tends to be deliberate in a way not all intentional action is. Indeed, deliberating about what to do is a major route to making judgments in the first place.

It is not easy to say what constitutes a judgment, but we should consider this briefly to set the stage for some of the points to come. Like the other intentional attitudes, judgment has (as already indicated) dispositional and occurrent forms. Judging that $p$ is true, in the sense of making a judgment to this effect, is occurrent; more specifically it is a kind of doing. Judging in this sense does not entail judging in the sense of appraising, where this is an action or activity: the action or activity of observing or focusing on something with a view to making a judgment about it. But one may also dispositionally judge—in the sense of simply holding the judgment—that another person is highly competent. Dispositional judgment is like dispositional belief in many ways; and in the common sense of the term—'holding the judgment'—it entails believing the proposition in question. (The converse entailment of course fails.)

Judging in the activity sense does not entail holding any belief of the kind broadly aimed at, say that Katherine's painting is the best in the gallery; but *making* the judgment that $p$ apparently does entail believing $p$, even if the belief is immediately lost, as where one instantly realizes that $p$ entails a false proposition or immediately sees decisive counterevidence to it. What is not altogether clear is whether making a judgment manifests the formation of belief produced by other things, such as the evidences being considered, or whether the judging itself normally produces belief. Both seem possible; and surely the latter may hold where the evidence seems to weigh about equally in favor of $p$ and some contrary, and the judging is like a push that gets the mind off the fence.

In moral matters, it is common to be, for some issues and for at least some time, on the fence: equally attracted to (or indifferent between) competing alternatives. Notoriously, prima facie obligations, such as promissory obligations and obligations of beneficence, sometimes conflict. This is emphasized by moral philosophers as different as W. D. Ross and John Stuart Mill.[7] Judg-

---

[7] See esp. chap. 2 of John Stuart Mill, *Utilitarianism*, ed. George Sher (Indianapolis, IN: Hackett, 1979), 24–25, in which Mill says, "There exists no moral system in which there do not arise unequivocal cases of conflicting obliga-

ment is often needed to arrive at a position on what one's final (preponderant) obligation is. What obligation is final is often unclear. We may need time to arrive at a belief, and often we make a judgment that something is so as a way of at once manifesting the formation of a belief and expressing that belief. As this suggests, making a judgment can be concurrent with forming a belief.

We can now see how intuitions and emotions can figure in yielding judgments of final obligation. Sometimes one option is intuitively right, but we withhold judgment and reflect, especially if the matter is important or we doubt whether we are right. Reflection can confirm or disconfirm our initial intuition, and such confirmation or disconfirmation is one route to moral judgment. Reflection may do this by evoking supporting or opposing intuitions, by leading us to a theoretical analysis, by providing premises that confirm or disconfirm the initial intuition, or in other ways. Reflection may also invoke emotion, though emotion may also be present initially. Moreover, emotions, for instance resentment and empathy, can pull in different directions, much as intuitions can. Take cases in which we consider the consequences of favoring one option over another. The thought of punishing a wrongdoer may yield a flush of gratification, but the thought of hurting the person might produce a guilty feeling that opposes the punitive inclination. Judgment that settles the matter may come only when an intuition or emotion (or both) favors a particular resolution.

---

tions . . . and there is no case of obligation in which some secondary principle is not involved" (25). What Mill calls secondary principles seem much like Ross's principles of prima facie obligation. Mill would deny their self-evidence but would agree with Ross in affirming (though on utilitarian grounds) the prima facie obligations in question.

In a sense, the kind of reflection I am describing, with its projection of consequences of what we do, is like using visual observation to get a better perspective on an object to be judged. If we are sufficiently foresightful, we can *see* what we should do. This is not moral perception; but it may be analogous, resting on grounds supplied by the imagination rather than by sense. For cases in which we are actually observing a situation of moral conflict, say where two people disagree on who should have a bequest, we may be able to achieve moral knowledge, partly based on moral perception, of what ought to be done, in this instance moral knowledge of who ought to receive the bequest. We might perceive wrongs on both sides, as where we see each wrong the other by lying; and, on seeing a good compromise realized in the writing of checks to the deserving parties, we might see how justice can be done. In either case, the theory of moral perception developed in this book is applicable: moral properties are consequential on the same kinds of properties whether the former are envisaged in projective imagination or discerned in an actual situation of human interaction.

Here again the analogy between moral and aesthetic judgment is instructive. We judge paintings and musical performances that are in our perceptual field, but we also judge imaginary plots not yet written and melodies sung only in the mind's ear. Intuition and emotion are relevant, as in the ethical case, though in the aesthetic realm emotion may be even more important, since a major function that is proper to at least some artworks is to please, to delight, or to evoke other feelings. Aesthetic pleasure can, however, be taken in what does not merit it, as moral approval and disapproval can also be misplaced. When are conditions optimal? David Hume's famous pronouncement on taste in aesthetic matters captures some of the major variables important in ethics as well:

> Strong sense, united to delicate sentiment, perfected by comparison, improved by practice, and cleared of all prejudice, can alone entitle critics to this valuable character . . . [and, he added] the joint verdict of such, wherever they are to be found, is the true standard of taste and beauty.[8]

The strong sense Hume speaks of is roughly the discriminative capacity that facilitates the formation of intuitions; the delicacy of sentiment he refers to bespeaks emotional sensitivity; and the comparisons he notes include the kind relevant in ethics.

As to the prejudice Hume warns of, I have not treated intuition, emotion, or moral judgment as immune to it. But the point that they are fallible must be balanced by another: in correcting them we must rely on elements of the same kind—intuitions. Sometimes the very content of an intuition is of a kind that can be judged only in an intuitive way. Do we, for instance, have obligations of self-improvement, or are reasons for self-improvement simply a matter of prudence? This cannot be answered apart from other intuitions—concerning, for instance, prudence, morality, what we "ought" to do whether we want to or not, and what is just a matter of self-interest rather than goodness or excellence.

---

[8] David Hume, "Of the Standard of Taste," reprinted in *Criticism: The Foundations of Modern Literary Judgment*, ed. Mark Schorer, Josephine Miles, and Gordon McKenzie (New York: Harcourt, Brace, and World, 1958), 446.

What we can also appeal to when conflicts arise for us among our intuitions, our emotions, or some combination of these, of course includes perception, our own and that of others. To be sure, perceptual responses to the world, like intuitions, are fallible; but we have seen good reason to think that moral perceptions are among the perceptions we may often rely on. They may evidence intuitions; they may justify emotions; and they often serve to anchor moral judgments in the objectively real world we share.

————

Emotion is not just a response to what we see, intuit, or judge. It may enable us to see more, it may evoke judgment, and it may provide evidence for judgment or intuition. Once we appreciate how discriminative and subtle emotions can be, we can see how, even on a single occasion, they may be mixed or even in conflict. When conflicts arise among our emotions, intuitions, or some combination of these, we can sometimes turn to perception, or recall its deliverances, to gain further information or refine information we have. Doing so may be fruitfully combined with exercising moral imagination to integrate our information and widen our sense of options. Our emotional responses to the world, like our sensory responses to it, are fallible; but moral emotions, like moral perceptions, are responsive to the properties that determine moral truths, and moral emtions and often reflect such truths. Moral emotions and moral intuitions may be both evoked and justified by moral perceptions; and those perceptions often provide a basis on which moral judgments can be refined and moral disagreements resolved. But emotions themselves, including certain non-moral ones such as anger and revulsion, may also yield moral justification for certain of our judgments. The same may be said of moral intuition. In complex matters, justified moral judgment may arise only when reflection takes account not just of general moral standards but also of our emotional and intuitive reactions to the acts, persons, or states of affairs we must appraise.

# Conclusion

IT IS TIME TO RECALL some major points that have emerged in this book. I have extended a detailed account of perception to the moral domain. Establishing that there is moral perception and that it is, like everyday observation of things around us, genuinely a response to the world supports the objectivity of ethics and the hope of improving cross-cultural understanding and communication. My theory of moral perception takes full account of the causal element in perception but does not require naturalizing moral properties, though, in virtually every detail, it is consistent with doing that if it should be possible. But the theory does require that moral properties have a base in the natural world. They are anchored in the natural world in a way that makes possible moral knowledge and the ethical objectivity that goes with it. The bridge from their naturalistic base to moral judgment often has the intelligibility of the self-evident, and under some conditions it has the reliability of necessary truth.

Moral perception is not a kind of simple perception in which moral properties are seen in the elementary way in which we see shapes and colors. Simple sensory perception of natural properties is at the core of moral perception; but it is *moral* properties that are seen in moral (visual) perception, and it is moral propositions that are perceptually seen to be true in many such cases. Many moral properties, then, are perceptible, though not, like color and shape, perceptual. Where moral properties are perceptible, moral propositions may be seen to be true in much the way many non-moral propositions may be seen to be true: on the basis of perceptually experiencing properties that ground their truth. Our moral perceptions are, moreover, a major route, though by no means the only route, to intuitions. Those perceptions may ground moral intuitions about what we perceive—actions, events, patterns, even persons themselves. Indeed, seeing that an act or a person has a moral property may itself be a manifestation of an intuitive perceptual capacity that has considerable discriminative subtlety regarding descriptive natural properties.

Intuitions are cognitive, but they may or may not be doxastic: they may be phenomenal seemings, a kind of impression of truth, rather than a kind of belief, though phenomenal seemings often yield belief and are not always clearly distinguishable from "occurrent" beliefs. Many intuitions of either of these cognitive kinds, like the perceptions that may underlie them, are responses to patterns, whether perceived, described, or simply imagined. An intuition may arise spontaneously; but many intuitions, far from being cognitive snapshots, may be formed only upon reflection, particularly where they are responses to complex patterns. The idea that intuitions are immediate reactions, or are more a product of feeling than of intellect, is a stereotype. There are many kinds of intuition. Some people, moreover, are more intuitive than others, as some are more logical; but the capacity for intuition, like the capacity for logical thought, is to some extent present in all normal human beings. In the light of all these points about intuition and moral perception, we can see both why moral disagreement is often inevitable and how it may often be resolved.

Moral intuitions and moral perceptions are commonly of wrongdoing, but they may also be of right-doing or of obligation, whether prima facie or final. The same holds for permissibility and other deontic notions and for axiological notions such as that of the intrinsically good. Whether a moral intuition ascribes a prima facie or overall status, the intuition may represent either a particular action, or a kind of act, as fitting, whether to another act, a judgment, an emotion, a human relationship, or something else again. An act may, for instance, be intuitively seen to be fitting either in relation to one element supporting it, as where it is (prima facie) obligatory simply in virtue of being promised, or in relation to a pattern of elements, as where, on the basis of the conduct indicated by many normative factors taken holistically in the situation, it is an overall obligation.

Self-evident propositions may also be objects of intuition, but they are not the only objects of it, nor its primary objects. Moreover, the view that we "just see" the truth of self-evident propositions is mistaken. The self-evident need not be obvious or even readily understandable, much less initially intuitive—even to someone capable of seeing its truth on reflection. The same holds for propositions that, like many singular moral propositions, are intuitive but not self-evident. What is self-evident is knowable without dependence on premises; but its internal constitution may require reflection before its truth can be seen.

Intuition may arise from emotion, but may also produce it. Neither entails the other: an emotion may have nothing to do with intuition, and an intuition may be unconnected with one's emotions. In moral matters, however, as in the aesthetic realm, there can be a kind of wisdom of the emotions: they can be rational responses to experience and can yield insightful intuitive judgment. Precisely because of the way in which emotions are often rational, discriminative responses to the properties on which moral properties are grounded, emotions may provide evidential support for intuitions. Perceptions are commonly crucial grounds for emotions, as they often are for intuitions. We often perceive facts or events that both evoke and justify emotions and intuitions. It is especially when intuitions reflect moral perceptions that they can evoke moral emotions or provide substantial evidential support for them, or both.

Without an emotional element, much intuition would not engage our motivational system as it does; and without emotion, our intuitions would be deprived of a major source of their supporting data. Without moral perception, the objectivity of our intuitions and of the moral judgments they produce, the objectivity of ethics overall, and the scope of moral knowledge would be greatly reduced. Moral perception not only yields moral knowledge; it also provides some of the raw material from which moral imagination constructs scenarios that help us both to arrive at moral judgments and to articulate ethical standards that can guide us in the future. Moral properties are in many cases perceptible elements in our experience, and a major task of normative ethics—a task that requires the efforts of us all—is to enhance the human capacity to discern those properties, to heighten our intuitive and emotional responsiveness to them, and to help us to make sound moral judgments in the light of them.

# Index

Alston, William P., 71n, 112n5
appearance, 19, 22–23; visual, 22–23
apprehension, 9, 86–90, 97, 114–15, 124; as, 89; aspectual, 88–90; capacity for 87; intuitive, 88, 97; that, 90
Aristotle, 78
Audi, Paul, xi, 108n
Austen, Jane, 78
Austin, J. L., 71n
awareness, 9, 13, 22–25, 28, 59, 61, 91, 116; direct, 9; higher-order, 23; intellective, 24–25; moral, 61; phenomenal, 24, 25, 28

Bagnoli, Carla, xi, 64n, 85n, 91n, 157n
Beanblossom, Ronald E., 19n12
belief: attributive, 20, 72–73, 126, 129; basing, 80; infer-ential, 66, 92–93; intuitive, 89, 92–93, 134, 144, 153; and judgment, 163–65; moral, viii, 25, 45, 49–52, 63, 70, 91, 113, 157; non-perceptual, 62; perceptual, 33, 52, 54, 60, 62–63, 65, 81, 99, 105, 112, 133; propositional, 54, 89, 126, 129–30
Bentham, Jeremy, 78

Berkeley, George, 21n14
Burge, Tyler, 13n5, 42n

causation, 26–28
Christensen, David, 74n
Churchland, Patricia Smith, 99n
cognition, ix, 3, 7, 33, 52, 61, 70, 78–80, 84, 98, 100–101, 104, 111, 113, 116, 123–24, 133, 135–37, 139–40, 144–45, 153, 156, 159, 161, 163, 171
conclusion of inference, 95–96, 144
conclusion of reflection, 95–95, 144
Confucius, 78
consequentiality, 35, 39, 55, 56, 59, 60, 106, 108, 117, 166. *See also* grounds
constitution, 43, 45, 55, 57–58, 63, 99, 124, 132, 134, 172
content, perceptual, 14–16; objectual, 15; property, 15; propositional, 15–16
Cook, Maeve, xi
Copp, David, 48n14, 55n, 57n5, 113n
Cornell realism, 55n
Crisp, Roger, xi, 76n4, 116n

Dancy, Jonathan, xi, 39n, 59n, 114n

D'Arms, Justin, 48n14, 57n5
defeasibility, 101
Deigh, John, 126n4
deliberation, 139, 158–59
De Oliveira-Souza, Ricardo,
141n
DePaul, Michael R., 113n
dependence: discriminative, 14,
69; epistemic, 61; inferential,
61; premise, 61
desire, 35, 130, 161–62
de Waal, Frans, 99n
Dickens, Charles, 78
disagreement, 65–66, 69–83, 95,
101, 103, 111, 166, 168, 172;
amoral, 74; attributional, 72–
73; content-specific, 72; gut
responses and, 83; illocutionary, 71–72, 74; indefinite, 71;
moral, 8, 65–66, 70, 74–77,
82, 103, 111, 149, 168, 172;
propositional, 72–73
discernment, 118–20, 135, 142.
*See also* responsiveness,
discriminative
discriminative responsiveness.
*See* responsiveness, discriminative
Dostoevsky, Fyodor, 78
Dreier, James, 114n
Dretske, Fred, 41n

Elgin, Catherine Z., 139n
Elster, John, 126n3
emotion, ix–x, 3–4, 48, 50, 66, 83,
85, 91, 121–61, 165–69, 172–
73; affective element in, 125–
27, 131; attributive, 128–29;
cognitive element in, 125–26,
130–31; conceptualization in,

128; dispositional, 131–32;
evolution and, 140–41; intentionality of, 127–29; internal
versus external roles of, 156;
and intuitions, 135–36, 153–
57; and judgments, 154–55;
moral, 123, 136–48, 168, 173;
motivational element of, 125–
27, 130–31; non-moral, 169;
occurrent, 131; propositional,
124, 128
empiricism, 99
epistemic parity, 75–80, 82,
100–101
Erlenbaugh, Joshua, 87n15
experience: emotional, 33, 122,
127; moral, 38–40, 56, 60, 99,
105, 116; perceptual, 14–16,
20–21, 24–26, 28, 37–38, 40,
48, 60, 105, 157; sensory, 21,
23–25, 38; visual, 11, 13, 15–
17, 20, 22, 25–27, 37–38
explanations, 8, 55, 109

Feldman, Fred, 116n
Feldman, Richard, 76nn4 and 5
Finn, Tracy, 91n, 122n, 141n
fitness. *See* survival value
fittingness, 40, 45–46, 54, 97, 138,
147, 148, 151, 159
Fricker, Miranda, xi

Gaut, Berys, 124n
Giaquinto, Marcus, 25n
Goldie, Peter, xi
Gordon, Robert M., 125n
Graham, Peter J., xi
Greco, John, 2n2, 19n11, 76n4,
113n
Greenspan, Patricia, 85n

grounds, viii, 7, 19, 32, 35, 39–44, 49–52, 55–56, 59–63, 65–66, 69, 79–81, 101, 106, 108, 113–20, 123–24, 134–35, 137, 166, 171, 173. *See also* consequentiality

Hagaman, Scott, xi
Haidt, Jonathan, 3n
hallucination, 11, 15, 20, 24–25, 90
Hernandez, Jill Graper, xi, 64n, 76n4, 113n
Holtzmann, Steven, 34n
Horgan, Terry, xi, 45n
Howard, Chris, xi
Huemer, Michael, 113n
Hume, David, 37, 102n, 162n, 167, 167n

illusion, 90, 97
imagination, 47
induction, intuitive, 86n
inference, 3, 21, 32, 34, 39, 46, 49, 51–56, 59, 61–62, 64–66, 81–86, 88, 92–93, 95–96, 101–2, 110, 117, 119–20, 129, 135, 138, 144–45, 155–56, 162
intuition, ix–x, 2–4, 46–48, 50, 65–66, 70, 80–106, 111–25, 127, 129–30, 133–45, 148, 153–61, 165–69, 171–73; apriority of, 65, 90, 95, 114–15, 118; attributive, 124; doxastic, 89, 91–92, 133; facultative, 87–88; moral, 70, 83, 85, 89, 91, 92, 96, 98–99, 103, 105, 113–17, 121–22, 133, 135, 139, 141–43, 156, 159–72; non-perceptual, 134–35; objectual,

86; philosophical, 96; propositional, 87; self-evident, 95; simple, 97
intuitionism, 3n, 44, 48, 64, 70, 76, 80–81, 85, 90, 113, 115; ethical, 44, 64, 70, 76, 80–81, 85, 113, 115
intuitive induction. *See* induction, intuitive
intuitiveness, 86–87

Jacobson, Daniel, 48n14, 57n5
judgment, 161–67; aesthetic, 103, 166; dispositional, 164; moral, ix–x, 1, 3–4, 8, 30, 32–33, 39, 61, 63, 71, 82, 106, 114, 121, 125, 131, 133, 137, 139–43, 149, 154, 156–58, 160–61, 165–70, 173; non-inferential, 129; non-moral, 33, 49, 140; singular, 30, 82, 120
justification, vii, ix–x, 4, 8, 19–20, 33, 51, 61–64, 70, 77–81, 83, 87, 90, 134, 137, 141, 144–45, 153–54, 168–69, 173; moral, 33, 63, 71, 119, 169; perceptual, 62–63; propositional, 144–45

Kaebnick, Gregory E., 139n
Kalderon, Mark Eli, 23n
Kant, Immanuel, 78, 150, 157n
Kennedy, Ralph, xi
knowledge: a priori, 25; empirical, 42; inferential, 52, 65, 119; intuitive, 44, 89, 100, 102, 118–19, 134; memorial, 46; moral, viii, ix, 1–5, 23, 30, 33, 44, 46, 51–53, 55, 57–66, 70, 81, 98, 100–102, 106, 116,

knowledge (*cont'd*)
119, 121, 133, 135, 137, 142, 154–55, 158, 170, 173; non-inferential, 46, 52; perceptual, 42, 45–46, 50, 58, 60–65, 70, 100, 102; premise-based, 61; testimony-based, 46. *See also* justification; perception; self-evidence

Lackey, Jennifer, 74n, 76n4
Lapsley, Daniel K., 3n, 141n
Lehrer, Keith, 19n12
Leich, Christopher 34n
Levinson, Jarrold, 109n
Locke, John, 38n, 48

Mall, Jorge, 141n
McBrayer, Justin, xi, 21n13
McCann, Hugh, xi
McDowell, John, 34n
McGrath, Sarah, 44n, 82n11
McKenzie, Gordon, 167n
Mele, Alfred R., 19n11, 76n4, 113n
Mi, Chienkuo, xi
Miles, Josephine, 167n
Mill, John Stuart, 78, 164, 164n
Miller, Richard W., 109n
Molyneux, Bernard, 87n15
Moore, G. E., 36n, 87n16
moral imagination, ix, 143, 148, 157–61, 166, 168, 173
moral principles, 4, 64, 81, 82, 85, 109, 115, 119, 146
moral realism. *See* realism, moral
motivation, 48, 74, 89, 98, 124–27, 137, 140, 142, 146, 148, 156, 173

Narvaez, Darcia, xi, 3n, 141n
naturalism, 1–2, 4, 8, 32, 55–57, 62, 64–65, 69–70, 141–42, 162, 170–71
Nida-Rumelin, Martine, 23n
Nöe, Alva, 48n13
non-cognitivism, 32–33
normativity, 2, 4, 8, 29, 37, 69, 101, 103, 107, 115, 117, 129, 146, 162, 172–73
Nuccetelli, Susana, 2n1
Nussbaum, Martha, 125n

objectivity, ethical, ix–x, 45, 56, 63, 65, 70, 82, 109, 170, 173
obligation, 2n1, 8, 30–31, 35, 40, 57, 64, 81–82, 86, 96, 101–2, 107–12, 114–19, 145–52, 164–65, 167, 172; final, 82, 102, 109, 118, 165, 172; of manner vs. matter, 151–53; overall, 82, 102, 109, 118, 165, 172; prima facie, 81–82, 96, 102, 109, 111, 115–16, 118, 121, 146, 151, 164–65, 172
organicity, 109
overdetermination, 157

Parfit, Derek, xi
peer, epistemic. *See* epistemic parity
perception: aspectual, 89; attributive, 10, 20, 53, 57, 89, 128; authority of, 8; basic, 58–59, 69, 93; belief and, 17–20; causal element in, 20, 25–29, 33, 42–43, 49, 55–56, 58, 60–62, 69, 126, 157; conceptualization in, 45–46, 54, 64; discrimination

in, 14, 19, 20, 39, 46, 53–54, 69, 145, 161, 167; factivity of, 10, 12–13; focal, 18; inner, 104; intellectual, 89; moral, viii–ix, 2–3, 9, 12, 17, 19, 21, 23, 25, 29–70, 81–83, 97–99, 103, 105, 113, 121, 125, 133–35, 137, 140, 142–43, 146–48, 157–61, 166, 168–73; of a moral phenomenon, 31, 44, 58, 103; peripheral, 18; phenomenology of, 12–14, 36–37, 44, 146; propositional, 10, 12, 20, 39, 47, 53, 57, 89, 113, 116, 135; representation in, 13, 37–38, 44, 48; sensory, 8–11, 21, 89, 170; simple, 10, 39, 50–51, 89, 97, 128, 170

perceptual content. *See* content, perceptual

perspectival disparity, 74

Prinz, Jesse, 57n5

properties: awareness of, 24–25, 28; base, 35, 38–39, 44–45, 56–57, 59–60, 69, 74, 100–101, 106, 108, 114–15, 117–19; descriptive, 107; dispositional, 132; intrinsic, 48; moral, 29, 31–36, 39–41, 44, 48–49, 55–57, 59–62, 64–65, 70, 74, 100–101, 105–7, 110, 113–15, 117–19, 121, 135, 166, 170–73; natural, 32, 55–57, 62, 69, 109, 170–71; perceptible, 32–35, 37, 41, 43–46, 49, 54, 56–67, 64–65, 70, 100, 119, 145, 171, 173; perceptual, 34–38; phenomenal, 14, 21–24, 28, 37, 38, 49; physical, 14, 21–23, 25

Railton, Peter, xi, 91n, 109n

rationalism, 2, 64, 99

rationality, 3, 19, 65–66, 70–71, 75–83, 85, 87, 91–95, 98, 114, 118, 122, 124, 137–39, 152–53, 156, 162, 173

realism, moral, 82

reflection, 54, 78–79, 81, 83–86, 88, 91, 95–86, 99, 104–6, 113–14, 119, 121, 144, 147, 151, 155, 159–60, 162–63, 165–66, 168–69, 171–73. *See also* conclusion of reflection

Reid, Thomas, 19n12

reliabilism, phenonmenological, 63–64. *See also* reliability

reliability, 32, 41, 43, 60, 63, 65, 78, 112–17, 120, 145, 161, 170; of intuition, 112–17, 161; of perception, 63n (*see also* seeing); phenomenological, 63

representation, 13–16, 20–21, 28, 33, 36–38, 43–45, 48, 54, 56, 58, 158; cartographic, 37–38, 56; pictoral, 37, 56

responsiveness, discriminative, 12–14, 18–19, 28, 30, 34, 39, 41, 43–44, 47, 49, 52–59, 62–63, 66, 79–80, 83–85, 89, 91, 93, 99–100, 104, 114, 116–20, 125, 134, 136–37, 139–43, 145, 147, 149, 151, 153–60, 168, 170–71, 173; emotions as, 137–40, 173

Roberts, Robert C., xi, 34n, 124n, 129n

Roeser, Sabine, 122n, 129n

Ross, W. D., 36n, 78, 86n, 118, 146n, 146–47, 151, 151n3, 164, 165n

Schleiermacher, Friedrich, 34n, 122n
Schorer, Mark, 167n
secondary qualities, 48–49
seeing, 9–17, 26–27, 36, 42–43, 52–53, 58, 89; apprehensional, 9; as, 11–12, 36, 89; and belief, 17–20; imaginational, 9, 47; indirect, 32; intellective, 9, 12, 15, 24–25, 33; moral, 43; perceptual, 9–10; proposi-tional, 13, 45, 52, 89. *See also* intuition; judgment.
seemings, 23, 46–47, 86–89, 91–93, 130, 133, 144, 171; intuitive, 46–47, 88–92, 130–33; non-doxastic, 92; percep-tual, 46–47; phenomenal, 144, 71; sensory, 91; that, 89. *See also* seeing
self-evidence, 2, 81–82, 87, 93–96, 104, 115, 165, 170, 172
Sellars, Wilfrid, 87n15
sense data, 22–24, 28
sensing, 22–24, 33, 40, 54, 92, 166; moral, 40, 166; phenom-enal, 92; visually, 22–23, 54
Shakespeare, William, 15n, 18n, 43, 108, 110–11, 124–25
Shea, Gary, 2n2
Sher, George, 164n
Sidgwick, Henry, 76n4
Siegel, Susanna, 16n7
Sinnott-Armstrong, Walter, xi , 91n, 113n

skepticism, ix, 2n2, 8, 20, 25, 30, 32–33, 60, 75, 77–82, 93, 113–14, 115; moral, ix, 8, 30, 32–33, 60, 75, 77–78, 81–82, 113
Smith, Michael, 56n
Smith, Quentin, 34n, 122n
Solomon, Robert C., 125n
Sosa, Ernest, xi
Stratton-Lake, Phillip, 36n
Sturgeon, Nicholas, 55n, 109n
supervenience, 107–8
survival value, 140–41

testimony, 7, 46, 70, 162
Thagard, Paul, 91n, 122n, 141n
Timmons, Mark C., xi, 19n11, 45n, 76n4, 113n
Tropman, Elizabeth, 48n14

unfittingness. *See* fittingness

Vyrynen, Pekka, xi

Wagner, Steven, 55n
Warfield, Ted A., 76nn4 and 5
Warner, Richard, 55n
Wedgwood, Ralph, 76n4
Whitcomb, Dennis, xi
Williamson, Timothy, 19n11
Wittgenstein, Ludwig, 34n
Wynn, Mark, 33n2, 122n

Zagzebski, Linda, xi, 125n
Zahn, Roland, 141n
Zimmerman, David, 55n